PORTFOLIO/PENGUIN

THE MESH

"The Mesh is the future of business—and Lisa Gansky describes it brilliantly! Read this book to find out what you need to do to be part of the new economy of the Mesh!"

—ALAN M. WEBBER, co–founding editor, *Fast Company*, and author of *Rules of Thumb*

"Networks exist only because of what you put into them, not what you take out. Lisa Gansky in *The Mesh* shows us why generosity is replacing greed as the central value of the emerging network economy."

—PETER SCHWARTZ, futurist; cofounder and chairman, GBN, and partner in the monitor group

"In this timely and extremely practical book, Gansky not only gives dozens of examples of sharing companies disrupting the status quo and experiencing exponential growth, but she also talks about why they're successful—what it means to be a Mesh business and what you have to do to thrive as the world moves to a share economy."

—JOHN LILLY, CEO, Mozilla

"Lisa Gansky has uncovered a revolution that even most of its perpetrators didn't know existed. It's a brave new marketplace, where consumers rule and business models are turned topsy-turvy. Where innovation and inspiration collide to create greener, cooler products and services that are high in value and values. And where disparate communities form, if only for an instant, to ignite companies and markets. The Mesh is an essential road map for tomorrow's winning companies and anyone who wants to create one."

—JOEL MAKOWER, executive editor, GreenBiz.com, and author of
Strategies for the Green Economy

"Since the '90s Lisa Gansky has had an uncanny knack for spotting, branding, and building businesses on the next big 'lifestyle' technologies. With The Mesh, she's branded one of the most significant economic trends ever, giving it a form that transcends the clichés of social media. And in typical Gansky style, she is using The Mesh to expand the Mesh. With the book and the Mesh directory, she's empowering people to connect with each other and build profitable, sustainable businesses together. How very meshy of her!"

—DENISE CARUSO, former *New York Times* technology columnist; senior research scholar, Carnegie Mellon University

"Gansky lucidly describes how a new generation of companies make their community's passion, intelligence, and resources a core part of the business itself. Kickstarter is honored to be included as part of this new movement."

—PERRY CHEN, cofounder and CEO, Kickstarter

"At thredUP, we fully embrace what Gansky calls the Mesh and are rapidly growing our service, community base, brand, and ecosystem around a new business model dedicated to extending the life of kids' clothing and making parents very happy!"

—JAMES REINHART, cofounder and CEO, thredUP

"Crushpad is a true Mesh business. Equal parts winemaking, Internet, and community involvement, Crushpad enables anyone with a true passion for wine to create their very own at the highest level. Gansky's book is a must-read for anyone who intends to create engaged fans and build strong brands."

—MICHAEL BRILL, founder and CEO, Crushpad

"This book offers a timely introduction to the reality and importance of Mesh companies—ones that provide products and services through sharing, via community participation and a culture of trust—in a way that really matters."

—CRAIG NEWMARK, founder of Craigslist

"Easy access to shared and personalized goods and services is going to be an integral and ubiquitous part of the new economy. Lisa has tapped into, explains, and explores this new phenomenon."

—ROBIN CHASE, cofounder and founding CEO, Zipcar

"*The Mesh* clearly reveals the dramatic shift enabled by our connected world. And Gansky's practical experience makes it real. It's essential reading for anyone in business."

—JOHN DONAHOE, CEO, eBay

THE MESH

Lisa Gansky has been a founder and CEO of multiple Internet companies, including GNN and Ofoto. She currently advises and invests in several social ventures, including New Resource Bank, Squidoo, Convio, TasteBook, MePlease, Slide, Instructables, and Greener World Media. She is a cofounder of Dos Margaritas, a conservation-focused social venture. She lives in Napa, California. Visit www.meshing.it.

The Mesh

Why the Future of Business Is Sharing

Lisa Gansky

PORTFOLIO / PENGUIN

PORTFOLIO / PENGUIN

Published by the Penguin Group

Penguin Group (USA) Inc., 375 Hudson Street,
New York, New York 10014, U.S.A.
Penguin Group (Canada), 90 Eglinton Avenue East, Suite 700,
Toronto, Ontario, Canada M4P 2Y3
(a division of Pearson Penguin Canada Inc.)
Penguin Books Ltd, 80 Strand, London WC2R 0RL, England
Penguin Ireland, 25 St. Stephen's Green, Dublin 2, Ireland
(a division of Penguin Books Ltd)
Penguin Books Australia Ltd, 250 Camberwell Road, Camberwell,
Victoria 3124, Australia
(a division of Pearson Australia Group Pty Ltd)
Penguin Books India Pvt Ltd, 11 Community Centre, Panchsheel Park,
New Delhi–110 017, India
Penguin Group (NZ), 67 Apollo Drive, Rosedale, Auckland 0632,
New Zealand (a division of Pearson New Zealand Ltd)
Penguin Books (South Africa) (Pty) Ltd, 24 Sturdee Avenue,
Rosebank, Johannesburg 2196, South Africa

Penguin Books Ltd, Registered Offices:
80 Strand, London WC2R 0RL, England

First published in the United States of America by Portfolio Penguin,
a member of Penguin Group (USA) Inc. 2010
This paperback edition with a new epilogue published 2012

10 9 8 7 6 5 4 3 2 1

THE LIBRARY OF CONGRESS HAS CATALOGED THE HARDCOVER EDITION AS FOLLOWS:
Gansky, Lisa.
   The mesh : why the future of business is sharing / Lisa Gansky.
      p. cm.
   Includes bibliographical references and index.
   ISBN 978-1-59184-371-9
   ISBN 978-1-59184-430-3 (pbk.)
   1. Lease and rental services.   2. Sharing—Economic aspects.   3. Information technology—
Economic aspects.   4. New products.   5. New business enterprises.   I. Title.
   HD9999.L4362G35 2010
   658—dc22
2010023606

Printed in the United States of America
Set in Joanna MT
Designed by Pauline Neuwirth

For my parents, Rose and Jack; my grandfather, Ben; and Chocolate and Suerte the lovely beings who have most shaped my worldview, offered unsolicited guidance, and inspired a deep spirit of sharing and openness.

And to all beings who are finding the balance between care for "the self" and care for our "shared self," our planet.

Contents

value of your customers' footsteps, or how can I make you never go?

The Mesh

Introduction

I was in Manhattan right around Christmas when an article about an L.A. landscaper named Scott Martin caught my eye. The recession was in full bloom, and Scott's business had been in the dumps. As reported in the *New York Times*, Scott wasn't one to get all that excited about Christmas, but there was one traditional sight that roused his ire. He hated seeing all the dead trees lying on the curb after the holiday, waiting to be hauled off to a landfill. Scott decided that this year, instead of just complaining about the waste, he would take advantage of it. As a landscaper, it would be simple for him to grow a stock of trees. Why not rent people living Christmas trees?

And that's exactly what he did. He set up a Web site offering cedars, pines, cypresses, and redwoods in various sizes at corresponding prices. He hired people with disabilities to tend to the stock. He offered customers eco-friendly ornaments. At the appointed time, Scott and a small crew, which included several of his laid-off pals, gamely put on reindeer antlers and delivered the trees to people's homes before the holiday. A couple of weeks later, he reversed the process. The crews picked up the trees, along with any wrapping paper to be recycled. Trees too big to save for the next season were donated to an urban reforestation project. The crew even offered to pick up their customers' Goodwill donations and drop them off. Talk about holiday spirit!

Scott Martin had figured out a clever way to *share* Christmas trees, and make money doing it. Instead of buying, owning, and then tossing a tree, his customers got access to their trees precisely when they wanted them. They had a greater variety of choices than the corner lots offered. The service was fast and convenient. Customers used Scott's site to pick their tree and delivery time (and one can easily imagine how mobile phones and tweets could sharpen the delivery details even further). No tying the tree to the roof of the car with bungee cords. No tripping and falling on the stoop and scratching your face. No wondering when the tree has become a fire hazard, figuring out the day for the city pickup, and dragging the needle-shedding tree carcass out to the curb. Customers could even take comfort in reducing their carbon footprint just a little.

Like Scott's business, this book is about a simple idea: some things are better shared. There is much to be said for owning things. But the dominant ownership mindset has often blinkered our business brains. The fact is that our commerce, not to mention our social lives, has always depended on sharing. When you start looking for them, "share platforms" are everywhere. During that holiday season in New York, essential shared goods and businesses seemed to jump out at me—hotels and apartment buildings, subways and taxis, airports and planes, churches and libraries. All the things that seemed to make New York . . . New York. Some are public, some private. The entire infrastructure—from the telephone lines and wireless networks, to streets and sidewalks, to public art and parks, to the legendary NYFD—is shared.

Some of history's cleverest business minds understood the

power of share platforms, from the aggressive titans who made fortunes building the nation's railroads to Conrad Hilton, who created the first premier brand of international hotels. Now, a new era of sharing-based businesses is beginning. Businesses as big as Netflix or Zipcar, and as small as a guy who rents Christmas trees, have figured out there is gold in giving people convenient access to shared goods.

These new share platforms differ in important ways from the type that profited Conrad Hilton. In Hilton's first few decades of operation, the communication infrastructure connecting the hotels to each other and to their customers—principally telephones and telegraphs—did not change much. Under that system, you called or wired to make a reservation for a nonnegotiable price. A clerk transcribed the information into the hotel's paper-based reservation system.

The new share-based businesses are bolstered and built on social media. Using Web-enabled mobile networks, they can define and deliver highly targeted, very personal goods and services at the right time and location. Today, using a pocket-size mobile phone, you can sit in a café while you map nearby hotel rooms, read reviews, play a video of the lobby and guest rooms, compare prices, negotiate a deal, request a recommended room, make a reservation, pay for the room, and generate directions to the hotel from where you're sipping your latté. In some places, your phone can send your location to a taxi service and find someone nearby who wants to share the cab. In the near future, the hotel's app may send you a bar code that offers you a room upgrade and a free drink and then opens the door to your suite, bypassing reception.

This shift represents much more than an improved reservation system. Up to now, the information revolution has primarily swept through industries and services that are or can be *digital*—numbers, text, sound, images, and video. Related sectors, such as banking, publishing, music, photos, and movies, have undergone massive change. Now, mobile networks are rapidly expanding that disruption to *physical* goods and venues, including hotels, cars, apparel, tools, and equipment.

That's possible because our GPS-enabled mobile devices move in real space and time with us. An Urbanspoon app on your phone, for example, can pick up your location and guide you to nearby recommended restaurants. The Craigslist app can help you quickly find a mechanic in a pinch. Physical goods are also electronically tracked by location and time—think of the UPS or FedEx tracking numbers that tell you where your package is at the moment. As a result, the network can connect us to the things we want exactly when we want them. We can increasingly gain convenient *access* to those goods, greatly reducing the need to *own* them. Why buy, maintain, and store a table saw or a lawn mower or a car when they are easily and less expensively available to use when we want them?

Mobile computing, enabled by GPS, WiFi, 3G, and Bluetooth, is growing at an explosive rate, and is expected to overtake desktop computing within only a few years. What's more, the game-changing expansion of Web-enabled mobile networks has converged with the explosion of social ones. Each reinforces the other. Within a historical eye-blink, we have constructed a whole new language of sharing. You text, poke, and tweet your friends to meet at the pub you chose on Yelp, and then share the evening's goofy photos on Facebook the hungover morning after. Awesome.

Something else has changed, too. The credit and spending binge that crashed the economy has left us with a different kind of hangover. We're increasingly conscious of how we've raced through our personal and environmental assets. We're forced to rethink what we care about. Throughout the world, we are reconsidering how we relate to the things in our lives and what we want from our businesses and communities. We need a way to get the goods and services we actually want and need, but at less cost, both personal and environmental. Fortunately, we're quickly gaining more power to do so.

For now, most companies stubbornly stick to various twists on a single tried-and-true formula: Create a product or service, sell it, and collect money. Just sell the guy a lawn mower and watch him walk out the door. Few businesspeople, including most entrepreneurs and venture capitalists, have imagined creating wealth any other way. Though they may use social media to market their products, their minds are still stuck in a 2-D buyer/seller/own-it world.

Around these entrenched businesses, a new model is starting to take root and grow, one in which consumers have more choices, more tools, more information, and more power to guide those choices. I call this emerging model "The Mesh." In recent years, thousands of Mesh businesses have been created and scaled up, a few into well-known brands. These businesses understand and cleverly exploit the perfect storm of mobile, location-based capabilities, Web and social network growth, changing consumer attitudes, and the historically understood market benefits of share platforms. In this book, I'll explore the ideas that underlie the myriad forms of the Mesh, and why it conveys extraordinary competitive advantages to entrepreneurs and businesses.

Fundamentally, the Mesh is based on network-enabled sharing—on access rather than ownership. The central strategy is, in effect, to "sell" the same product multiple times. Multiple sales multiply profits, and customer contact. Multiple contacts multiply opportunity—for additional sales, for strengthening a brand, for improving a competitive service, and for deepening and extending the relationship with customers. Using sophisticated information systems, the Mesh also deploys physical assets more efficiently. That boosts the bottom line, with the added advantage of lowering pressure on natural resources. Not always and not for everything, but a Mesh network that manages shared transactions has the growing capacity to soar past a company that sells something once to one owner. All of us reap the rewards of dramatically improved service and choice at a lower personal cost.

This has been my life's work: how to get more real value for people by leveraging the Web as a sharing platform. In 1993, I had the terrific good fortune to work with Dale Dougherty and Tim O'Reilly in creating GNN, the first commercial Web site. We designed the first online transaction and ran the first ads on the Web. We helped unleash the Internet revolution, which uprooted and reconfigured most major industries and business models, displaced leading brands, and forced the redesign of hundreds of key products. We sold GNN to AOL.

A few years later, I saw a very young boy at O'Hare mimicking taking a photograph with his fingers. Instead of holding his "viewfinder" up to his eye, he held it out in front, like a view screen. There it was. Digital images were clearly the future. Using the Web, here was an opportunity to turn the business of sharing and printing photos on its ear. Kamran Mohsenin and I began riffing about a better, faster, and less wasteful model. Those conversations led to the creation of Ofoto.

Ofoto used the Web's rich and growing digital infrastructure to share photos through people's social networks of family, friends, and colleagues. As we hoped, Ofoto became very profitable while generating far less waste than the traditional film model. We sold Ofoto to Eastman Kodak, where it became the company's core digital photo service. We grew to be the largest online photo sharing and printing service in the world, with well over 40 million customers.

Over the last several years, I've continued to bring a variety of Web and mobile services to market, while sustaining a concern about nature and communities. During my career, I have worked with the founders of Yahoo!, AOL, Google, PayPal, and Mozilla. Again and again I've watched the same process unfold: an innovator sees a new opportunity, exploits it, inspires others, and we all benefit.

In this fast-moving environment, it has become an essential business skill to recognize, well ahead of your competitors, the discontinuity that generates new platforms, models, expectations, and brands. See it first. Act. Win.

The Mesh is that next big opportunity—for creating new businesses and renewing old ones, for our communities, and for the planet. And it's just beginning.

Getting to Know the Mesh

WHAT'S HERE: two parts data and a pinch
of social; better things, easily shared;
wear your mesh lenses; my date with mini
mucho; welcome to the mesh buffet.

"**What's good for** General Motors is good for the country," CEO Charles E. Wilson bragged to a Senate subcommittee in 1953. Although popular cartoonist Al Capp subsequently used the comment to satirize Wilson as "General Bullmoose," the boast was not unfounded. GM reigned for decades as the titan of the leading industry, envied for its brand and business model. Three years after Wilson testified, Fortune magazine began publishing their list of the five hundred largest corporations in the United States. General Motors came out on top, and stayed there for the next twenty years. For another twenty-six years, GM vied with two other auto-related corporations, Exxon and Ford, for the top spot. When GM was forced to beg Congress for a bailout in late 2008, and then went into bankruptcy, it drew the curtain on an industrial model, centered on cars, that had dominated business for much of the twentieth century.

Meanwhile, far from the national spotlight, a different kind of car company was quietly breaking business records. That company, Zipcar, had established itself in less than nine years throughout the United States, Canada, and Europe. From its inception in 2001, Zipcar had one of the decade's fastest growth rates. Revenues doubled and tripled in the second and third years. In 2009 it generated over $130 million in revenue, up over 30 percent from the previous year.

Zipcar is a near perfect example of a successful Mesh business. It doesn't make, sell, or repair cars. It shares them. The Boston-based company was the brainchild of two friends who first met while their children were in kindergarten. While sitting in a café in Berlin in 1999, Antje Danielson saw signs for a service that shared cars. She became interested and then enchanted. She discovered that the service was easy to use and made enormous sense. Unlike traditional rental car companies—an old-fashioned share platform—the cars could be conveniently located and distributed throughout the city. You could locate and reliably reserve the precise car you wanted on the Web, and use it for an hour or for a day or more. That made the service practical for ordinary day-to-day use, not just for travel.

When she returned to Cambridge, Antje shared her discovery with her friend, an MIT business school grad. "A lightbulb went off in my head," says Robin Chase today. "I thought: This was what the Internet was made for." From that conversation, the two made plans to launch what was to become the largest car-sharing service in the world.

learning to conjugate Zip.

Zipcar's founding wasn't always a smooth ride. First, the pair had to face down the doubters. When they pointed to the runaway success of car sharing in Switzerland, potential funders were dismissive. "Now car sharing seems commonplace," Robin says. "But at the time the venture capitalists told us, 'Well, that's the Swiss, but it will never work here.'" Ironically, many years later she would hear from a business group in Paris: "Sure, that works fine in America, but it will never take off in France."

Zipcar's first car was a brand-new VW Beetle, a model that had just reentered the market. The company founders deliberately picked brands different from those the rental car companies supplied, and gave each car a name. They dubbed that first Beetle "Betsy." The name was practical for identifying an individual vehicle, and helped bond the customers with the car and brand. They called their customers "Zipsters" and gave each a membership "Zipcard," a hip-looking, wallet-size plastic card. They made sure the cars were clean, well maintained, well located, and in every way reliable. And from early on, Zipcar grew at a brisk pace, and acquired competitors. It invested in Avancar in Spain, and took over Streetcar in the U.K., to become the fastest-growing car-sharing network in Europe. Zipcar based this success on a simple formula: Create an easy and efficient way for people to share cars rather than own them. The service is convenient, fast, and affordable.

it's about information, not transport.

The company's founding team included Roy Russell, who is Robin's husband, as the tech lead. Russell designed the IT infrastructure, which was built to scale up, yet excruciatingly attentive to every detail of marketing, technology, and operations. The details included things like how and when the cars would be washed, finding and negotiating just the right parking spots at the right cost, and figuring out the basic rules that drivers would find reasonable, and honor. The robust information platform and focus on building the brand distinguished Zipcar from early car-sharing companies that were merely long on good intentions, many of which failed.

In fact, Zipcar is primarily an information business that happens to share cars. The company collects information about who is using the car, and when, how, and where it's being used. That data makes the business work and generates the greatest value. As the number of people using Zipcar grows, the collected data enables the company to better know specific groups of customers, defined by demographics or location. That in turn creates opportunities to extend the brand to, say, bikes or clothes. Other services can be offered directly by the car-sharing company or its partners. Over time, Zipcar has developed partnerships with food and wine, hotel, fitness, and even ink cartridge recycling companies. Ancillary services might include traffic and transit advice, restaurant reservations, suggested local events, or help in finding gear for your journey. In Portland, Zipcar has outfitted a couple dozen of their cars with bike racks, and partnered with state and national parks to offer free passes.

Each new service creates opportunities to grow with like-minded business partners. As this "ecosystem" of businesses grows, the network delivers better, more personalized services to customers. And when customers appreciate the service, they tell their friends. Zipcar has built a brand, challenged formerly entrenched business models, and helped create a new category in personal transportation. A measure of its success is that Hertz, Enterprise, and Daimler have all launched car-sharing services. But Zipcar remains the largest car-sharing company, and recently filed an initial public offering for raising additional funds to scale the service.

my date with mini mucho.

Although Zipcar appealed to me as an entrepreneur, I always want to understand a business from the perspective of a customer. What will it take to win me over and keep me long-term? Honestly, when I first became aware of car-sharing services, I disregarded them. I had friends in San Francisco who swore by them, but I wasn't ready emotionally to let go of my car. I figured it was fine for other people. I was like my friend the surgeon who would always tell his frightened patients, "It's minor surgery." But once I found him in a corridor in the hospital, standing outside his office, and he looked like crap. I said, "Michael, what's wrong?" He said, "Well, I have to get such-and-such kind of surgery." I said, "Well, that sounds like minor surgery." And he pulls me really close and he says, "Screw you, Gansky! Minor surgery is when we do it to somebody else."

The Mesh, to work, can't just be for "somebody else." It has to be for me, and people like me. So I tried my first Zipcar, on a trip to Vancouver, where I fell in love with a little two-door number named Mini Mucho.

Before I left the Bay Area, I signed up for a membership on the Zipcar Web site. They have several different flavors for joining, including what I call the "tapas" version—trial choices like "I'm not really sure if I like it or not, so I'm going to try it first." In a few days I received my member's Zipcard in the mail. Today, you can also download the Zipcar app on your mobile phone. Your Zipcard or app-enabled phone unlocks the car by wirelessly connecting to a box under the windshield that contains a circuit board, processor, and modem. When you make a reservation, your card or app is authorized for that specific car, using AT&T's wireless network. The same network allows Zipcar to remotely monitor the vehicle.

Once I knew when and where I'd be staying in Vancouver, I could see which cars were available close to my hotel. The Web listings are organized by location and inventory. Let's say you need a station wagon, or you really want a hybrid, figuring it would be a great way to test-drive the car. Or perhaps your main concern is that the car be parked nearby. Either way, you can view the options. For my trip, I wanted something super convenient. I didn't have that much gear, so a small car was fine. On the Web site, I saw a photo of Mini Mucho, which was parked just two blocks from my hotel, and made my reservation.

After arriving in Vancouver, I checked in to my hotel and then walked around the corner to a neighborhood garage. Unlike with a car rental, I didn't have to go back to the airport, or some place that's crazy far away, and then come back into the city again. There's no hard-to-find exit at the airport to return a car. Car-share parking is optimized for convenience. I quickly found Mini Mucho, which was a fabulously ridiculous, visible-from-Seattle shade of yellow.

I was offered an online orientation for using the car beforehand, but it's not tricky, not even the first time. I took the Zipcard, which has an embedded chip, out of my wallet. When I held it to the windshield, the card unlocked the car. The keys were there, Mini Mucho was all gassed up, and a credit card for filling up the car before returning was tucked in the visor. It was a lovely, easy experience.

As I drove Mini Mucho all over the place, I became attached to her. And giving the car a name worked its magic on me. If I lived in Vancouver or I was going back again, I would seek Mini Mucho out. It was super fun. Knowing your vehicle carries some of the perks of ownership and takes any unpleasant surprises out of the equation. The experience was very different from renting with Hertz, or one of the other big car rental companies, where you're only allowed to pick a category of car—small, medium, or large—like a Slurpee.

While in Vancouver, I also tried out the local bike-sharing service. The city is one of the best places in the world to ride a bike. For bike sharing, a credit card in a slot usually unlocks a bike. You ride your bike around and return it to the same rack, or to another one elsewhere. (Barcelona even has a phone app now that tells you which of the four hundred return stations is closest.) In Vancouver, the bike-sharing locations are concentrated near the park and near public transportation. The paths are impressive, and you can take the bicycle on the ferry.

one part net. two parts data.
more than a pinch social.

Vancouver is home to a wealth of Mesh-style businesses and organizations. I visited food co-ops, beautiful boutique stores organized and run by a segment of their customers. Through a friend, I got an inside look at innovative urban design features enabling people to walk, bike, or find convenient public transportation around the city. I got a tour of the much-remarked-upon green buildings and transport systems constructed for the winter Olympics. But Vancouver is not unique. Thousands of Mesh businesses are springing up around the globe, in the Americas, Europe, Middle East, and Asia.

Mesh businesses are thriving on the growth of social media, the Internet, wireless networks, and mobile phones. They use data crunched from every available source to deliver high-quality goods and services to people only when they need and want them. Mesh businesses share four characteristics: sharing, advanced use of Web and mobile information networks, a focus on physical goods and materials, and engagement with customers through social networks. Of course, not every business or organization discussed in this book contains every element. Like any large, rapidly growing advance, the Mesh expresses itself in a variety of ways along a continuum. Some businesses start in Full Mesh mode. Many, many others are moving in the right direction.

What characterizes a Mesh business?

1. The core offering is something that can be **shared**, within a community, market, or value chain, including products, services, and raw materials.

2. **Advanced Web and mobile data networks** are used to track goods and aggregate usage, customer, and product information.

3. The focus is on shareable **physical goods**, including the materials used, which makes *local* delivery of services and products—and their recovery—valuable and relevant.

4. Offers, news, and recommendations are transmitted largely through word of mouth, augmented by **social network services.**

Why call this new wave of businesses "The Mesh"? A Mesh describes a type of network that allows any node to link in any direction with any other nodes in the system. Every part is connected to every other part, and they move in tandem. To me, "The Mesh" is an apt and rich metaphor to describe a whole new phase of information-based services. Mesh businesses are knotted to each other, and to the world, in myriad ways. Some connections are formed directly, such as an agreement among companies to identify a market and make coordinated offers. These companies share information to facilitate access to new customers, customer preferences, and goods. Other connections are formed indirectly through third parties, such as aggregated consumer data or via customers' social networks.

The Mesh is made possible by the way in which we are all increasingly connected to everything else—to other people, businesses, organizations, and things. This is the first time in human history when this kind of far-reaching, always-on, and relatively inexpensive connectivity has existed. Just as our minds are more than a collection of neurons, these Mesh connections have given rise to something more complex and challenging. In the brain, all the parts—DNA, nerve cells, and lobes—are constituent of each other and in constant communication. We can likewise describe the Mesh in terms of its multiple parts, such as electrons, mobile devices, servers, services, partners, and customers. But like our minds, the Mesh is much greater than the sum of its parts. Now that everyone and everything is becoming connected to everyone and everything else—Twitter reached 50 million tweets a day in February 2010—something new has been born that is constantly growing and adapting. The Mesh has a clear pulse. And it's a fast learner.

Even before the rise of the Mesh, the Web had ingested, dissolved, and reshaped hundreds of industries and tens of thousands of businesses, communities, teams, and expectations worldwide. As a Web entrepreneur, I've watched old business models and brands tumble one after another. From publishing to retailing to banking, companies have been forced to adapt or die. Amazon grabs the bookselling market from Borders, Barnes & Noble, and Blackwell. It marches on to become the world's biggest online retailer, and then to further disrupt the publishing industry by introducing the Kindle and widespread access to e-books. Song sharing via the iPod and iTunes transformed the music industry. Ofoto created a platform for sharing digital photos that Kodak was compelled to embrace and that helped inspire other digital share platforms. Industries and brands that once seemed bigger than life and eternal are now scrambling to find a new way forward. Many were already in a free fall when the recession gave them an extra shove into the spiral of doom. Dozens of industries and brands that once seemed indestructible are now struggling to find solid footing in a changing world.

better things. easily shared.

To date, the biggest disruptions have occurred in businesses that largely involve digital products and services, such as music or financial data. The Mesh enables businesses to also profit handsomely by streamlining access to physical goods and services. These businesses are relatively easy to start and are spreading like wildfire: bike sharing, home exchanges, fashion swap parties, energy cooperatives, shared offices, cohousing, music studios, tool libraries, food and wine cooperatives, and many more. They leverage hundreds of billions of dollars in available information infrastructure—telecommunications, mobile technology, enhanced data collection, large and growing social networks, mobile SMS aggregators, and of course the Web itself. They efficiently employ horizontal business to business services, such as FedEx, UPS, Amazon Web Services, PayPal, and an ever-increasing number of cloud computing services. All the Mesh businesses rely on a basic premise: when information about goods is shared, the value of those goods increases, for the business, for individuals, and for the community.

Mesh businesses are legally organized as for-profit corporations, cooperatives, and nonprofit organizations. Once I started looking, I quickly uncovered over 1,500 relevant companies and organizations. The Mesh, I realized, was further along than I had originally imagined. In less than a decade, the Mesh model has infiltrated dozens of categories, including fashion, real estate, energy, travel, entertainment, transportation, food, and finance. The shift to the Mesh is quietly changing the way business is done, and it's picking up speed.

Mesh businesses come in all shapes and sizes, including extra large. Netflix, for example, is a share platform that transformed the video and film distribution industry. The company posted $1.36 billion in sales in 2009 and a $4.76 billion market cap in 2010, only a few years after displacing the reigning company in video rentals (more about that in chapter 8). Netflix has inspired similar models elsewhere, including Seventymm, a similar service in India that offers movies in eighteen Indian and foreign languages.

Other Mesh businesses take advantage of local resources. Crushpad helps wine lovers experience the joys of selecting, crushing, fermenting, and blending their own Napa varietals with the help of seasoned wine pros, and at substantially less cost than buying their own equipment. Several of their customers have created custom labels that are sold on the site.

put on your Mesh lenses.

Sometimes, as Crushpad's Michael Brill discovered, Mesh opportunities reveal themselves when you're paying attention. It helps to put on what I like to call your "Mesh lenses." Look around you for physical resources that could be more efficiently and profitably shared using information networks. When you see in this new way—through Mesh lenses—rich and surprising business opportunities reveal themselves, even in your immediate surroundings. Ask yourself how you might reduce the burdens of ownership, such as storage, insurance, maintenance, and disposal.

Crushpad Wine

When Michael Brill ripped up his backyard and installed two dozen grapevines at his home in San Francisco, it was, he said, by far the coolest thing he'd ever done. While Brill was making the wine in his garage, people walking by stopped to help. At the season's high production point, one hundred people popped in to lend a hand, have some pizza and beer, and get their clothes dirty. By accident, he had tapped into a latent passion in many people to make their own wine.

Inspired by this experience, in 2004 Brill started Crushpad. The company is targeted to people, like his volunteers, who want to make their own wine but don't own a vineyard. Crushpad provides everything they need, including high-quality grapes, access to wine experts, and crushing, fermentation, and bottling facilities. Brill, now the CEO, thought the primary business would come from restaurants, bars, and retailers who wanted their own wines and labels. But it soon became clear that no restaurant—always cash-tight on low margins—was going to pay $10,000 for a private wine label that they wouldn't see for two years. Today, Brill laughs. "That model was *so* not going to work."

Instead, the company figured out there were a lot of people who wanted to make fifty to a hundred cases a year. Today, anyone can make a barrel of wine using Crushpad's tools and metrics, including fermentation data and information for interpreting it. The Crushpad customer base remains passionate. Many of them fly in for the crush. The company offers a fairly low price point for beginners and provides lots of assistance. For those far away, it sends barrel tastings. For those who only want to blend wine, it sends a case of six small wine bottles (splits) and a graduated cylinder, and you add different volumes of claret, pinot noir, and cabernet until you come up with your preferred blend. Through Crushpad Commerce, customers not only make wine but sell it under their own brand. The company offers a platform for creating a customized Web site with the feel of a big winery. There, wine lovers can order fabulous Napa wines for a nice price.

Crushpad offers access to materials and tools that are too expensive and involved for most people to own. Starting with 5,000 square feet of space, the company now has ten times that much. As Crushpad has grown, Brill has started investigating what's been learned by music providers such as Pandora, Rhapsody, or MOG about how to create "influencers" that help people discover new music. Who are the influencers for wine purchases? Retail store staff? Magazines and blogs? Restaurant sommeliers? These are exactly the kinds of questions that can help a Mesh business take off.

If you're like most of us, there are many things you now don't use, or use infrequently, such as musical instruments, specialty sporting equipment, or a second car. You may own them for the convenience of having them available, just in case, or possibly to impress friends. Imagine how much wasted money and time they represent. (Some sites, such as wattzon.com and carbon-neutral.com, will actually calculate it for you.) Consider how much you'd save or earn if it were easy and secure to share the stuff you seldom use. Mesh businesses turn that potential into profit, much the same way that people rent out a second home when not using it. You just have to "see" it.

Of course, not everything can or will be shared. That's an extreme. I'm not looking at the extreme. I'm looking for where you get a big payoff for a family, for a community, for a business, and for the planet by reducing the friction of sharing. Zipcar succeeds, for example, because the value proposition of car sharing is compelling. Cars sit unused twenty-three hours a day, on average, and many families own more than one. Through car sharing, a person in the United States saves an average of $400–600 monthly on insurance, maintenance, and other costs. Dense urban areas, where car sharing is most efficient, can gradually free up valuable parking and street space for public and private use. And a UC Berkeley study found that members of one car-sharing service drove 47 percent less after joining. As a result, the car-share service saves 20,000 pounds of carbon dioxide emissions each day. That's a big payoff.

yours sometimes. own-to-mesh.

Zipcar is what I call a Full Mesh model, meaning that the company owns and maintains the vehicles. By participating, I get the benefits associated with owning, but without the hassles and cost.

own to mesh

use a little

use a lot

frequency of use

cost

$ $$$$

{ not meshy }

mesh sweet spot

{ not meshy }

{ not meshy }

The Mesh Sweet Spot: High Cost, Infrequently Used Goods.

Roomorama

Jia En Teo and Federico Folcia met on the job at Bloomberg in New York City and quickly discovered a mutual interest in travel. To help fund their habit, they rented out their apartments, primarily through Craigslist, while exploring the world. The drawback: Jia and Fede had to sift through hundreds of responses to their ads and deal with complicated and separate payment systems. They realized that many hosts and guests alike could benefit from a more convenient way to arrange short-term stays while traveling. So in 2008 they ditched their corporate gigs and launched Roomorama.com—a stress-free peer-to-peer platform for making your home (or second home) a short-stay time-share.

From New York, Roomorama has spread to Barcelona, London, Los Angeles, Paris, and Vancouver. The booking process is simple and secure: all payments occur online. Hosts know that their guests will pay in advance, and guests rest assured that their money is in safe hands (the money isn't released to the host until the renter verifies that the room was accurately advertised). There is no risk for either party.

By early 2010, 1,500 apartments in New York and over 4,000 listings across the country were available to travelers through Roomorama. The company gained early support by making customer-suggested improvements to the site, such as their "Shoutout" feature. There, renters can send an e-mail to prospective hosts with a last-minute plea to lower the rental price. Maybe the renter can only pay $70. A host who charges $85 per night has the option to meet the request or not.

The company continues to grow, sometimes in unexpected ways. As home prices dropped over the past year, one member saw an opportunity to acquire almost a hundred properties and list them on Roomorama. He's become a hotelier of sorts, using Roomorama's reservation platform and collection service. This is what a Mesh marketplace like Roomorama does. In providing a service, it creates opportunities for everyone. Will businesses like this one become the future of the hospitality industry? Or unveil convenient ways to secure more value from real estate? What will services like this mean for traditional hotels or households?

Many of the Mesh businesses operate in this way, making the capital investment and deriving their profit from micro-leasing arrangements facilitated by information networks. Other businesses use an Own-to-Mesh model. They create a platform for people who own things to share them easily and profitably. VRBO (Vacation Rental by Owner) and Roomorama, two home-sharing services, are good examples of Own-to-Mesh businesses. You own your home, but can Mesh it when you travel.

In Own-to-Mesh models such as Roomorama, income often derives from transaction fees and partnership deals. Certain car-sharing services also profit from the Own-to-Mesh model by charging transaction fees. RelayRides, a company in Baltimore, has created a platform for people who own cars to micro-lease them to other people. The company underwrites the insurance risk, creates mechanisms for evaluating prospective users, and provides a platform for tracking the cars and matchmaking among car owners and users. WhipCar, in the U.K., DriveMyCarRentals, in Australia, and SprideShare, in the Bay Area, also Mesh owners' vehicles. Divvycar provides tools and support to anyone who wants to share their own car—or anything else, including boats, bikes, and tools. All of these companies illustrate a key advantage of the Mesh—the opportunity for customers to lower costs and derive more value through network-enabled sharing.

Both the Full Mesh and Own-to-Mesh models are most successful when the customer feels empowered by relinquishing or sharing ownership. Mesh businesses are well positioned to constantly improve their customers' convenience by refining the overall experience, while offering them long-term savings and near-term happy surprises. Those ingredients will make sharing irresistible—customers will choose access to superior goods and services over living with lots of stuff. Not so long ago, stuff was all the rage. But what's so fabulous about piles of poorly built possessions, hardly used or maintained, and hard to find when you need them? (Which sort of describes my garage.)

profit? show me.

Market leaders view Mesh businesses as expanding and engaging new models for bringing services or products to market. Hundreds of millions of dollars in venture funding have already flowed into the Mesh. Thriving Mesh companies like Zopa, Prosper, Lending Club, Zipcar, Kickstarter, thredUP, SmartyPig, Etsy, Instructables, and smava were all funded by well-respected, big-name venture funds.

Early in my research, I talked with Chris Larsen of Prosper and Giles Andrews of Zopa, leading peer-to-peer lenders. I spoke with Lucy Shea of U.K.-based Futerra, creators of Swishing and founders of the fashion exchange concept; Robin Chase, cofounder of Zipcar; Shelby Clark, founder of RelayRides; Sunil Paul, creator of Spride Share services; Perry Chen, the founder of Kickstarter, a community of artists and funders; James Reinhart of thredUP; Derek Sivers, inventor of MuckWork, hosted services for musicians; and Jia En, cofounder of Roomorama. I got a sense of what drives these entrepreneurs and the sort of trends they're seeing in their businesses, from customers, partners, and investors. I also spoke to senior executives from large corporations such as GE, Target, HP, Best Buy, Flextronics, and Nissan. They, too, are seeking the ability to respond to markets more quickly, with thoughtfully designed products and services that enable access. In some cases, these industry behemoths have radically shifted ways of addressing partners and customers. Others are actively developing more efficient systems for sharing materials and natural resources. Mesh businesses are attracting attention, gaining momentum, and drawing competitors—blending all the ingredients for a frothy new platform. It's big, growing, and timely.

whoa! what's driving this thing?

The Mesh arrives just in time. Powerful forces drive it. From a business standpoint, we have already mentioned how the rapid growth of mobile and social networks energizes the Mesh model. These allow for more efficient and more personalized access to products and services. But there are also four global trends that favor the Mesh, all of which will be discussed at greater length in chapter 3.

First, the economic crisis has created a deep distrust of older brands and models. Historically, such times favor the emergence of new companies and the remaking of old ones. And indeed, there's considerable evidence that consumer attitudes are changing in response to the crisis, including a willingness to try new brands. Second, in the wake of the crisis, consumers are rethinking what they consider valuable in their lives. This is an opening to new models for delivering products and services that offer more value at less cost.

Population and resource pressures also drive the Mesh. Climate change and depleted natural resources are rapidly increasing the cost and risk of doing business the old way. The global population will expand to 9 billion people by mid-century, just as critical resources, including land, potable water, and oil, are shrinking. Simple math suggests that in order to have a peaceful, prosperous, and sustainable world, we are going to have to do a more efficient job of sharing the resources we have. Pragmatic and visionary businesspeople and governments understand this, and are reorienting themselves accordingly. The companies, cities, and countries that get there first will define business success in the early twenty-first century. That's why the so-called clean tech and renewable energy sectors are hot on several continents. Or why policy experts are debating the best way to develop a "smart grid" that will transform the way energy is generated and shared.

Finally, world population growth has sped up the trend toward greater urban density, which favors Mesh businesses. A car- or bike- or tool-sharing business can offer a greater depth and variety of products and services in neighborhoods where there are more people nearby to take advantage of them.

As an entrepreneur, I'm excited to have a new platform to reinvent markets and create thriving, customer-loving businesses. But I'm also thankful for new approaches that are good for the planet and its inhabitants. The Mesh yields what is sometimes called the "double bottom line"—greener commerce and greater profits (or triple if you add in the social benefits). The ethic of doing well while doing good has already created wildly successful companies such as Patagonia, Triodos Bank, The Body Shop, and Virgin Group. Elite business schools at UC Berkeley, Stanford, Harvard, Babson, Columbia, Oxford in the United Kingdom, INSEAD in France, McGill in Canada, IE in Spain, EGADE in Mexico, and other top universities devote curriculum to social entrepreneurship and sustainable business. Tomorrow's business leaders recognize that using resources efficiently increasingly drives profit, and that trust in a business's environmental and social practices increasingly drives informed consumers' decisions.

growing the mesh ecosystem.

From the business-to-business side, I also appreciate the rich partnership opportunities. I look at Mesh businesses as a kind of ecosystem. They can be organized around classes of things that people want to do, like transportation and travel. They can be organized around a profile centered on a demographic (age, gender, region, and so on) or psychographic (extreme sporter, foodie, cultural creative, and so forth). Partnership businesses will join the ecosystem and provide a domain of products or services to like-minded audiences. The voice, package, and price point must make sense for that market. Interesting services can be exclusively targeted with limited-time offers. For example, I recently noticed that Taxi Magic (a national taxi dispatch service with a mobile app) had teamed up with Heineken to promote safe journeys home. The partnership is a natural fit. It's "on brand" for both parties and will expand to other types of transit and activities over time.

New businesses have formed for that purpose, including Groupon, foursquare, Gowalla, Feest, and MePlease. As one example, Groupon leverages a traveler's buying power by enabling groups of people to get discounts on selected services and products. Let's say they are offering a huge discount for a bus charter to Yosemite, but you must collect ten people to take the deal. Mobile devices facilitate passing the offer along to friends and acquaintances to quickly assemble your group. Groupon offers you a place to find the forty other people you need for the per-ticket price to make sense for everyone. Groupon is similar to a buying club, but one that uses the Web and mobile devices to enable merchants to create time-specific offers for impromptu groups. Started in Chicago in late 2008, Groupon spread to thirty cities, quickly became profitable, and recently received $135 million in new funding.

It's easy and fun to imagine potential partnerships. A car-sharing service, for example, might craft a deal with Whole Foods, Blue Shield, and SmartyPig. Here's a scenario: If you spend over $100 a week with Whole Foods, you're entitled to a free car for a half day a week. Blue Shield, recognizing that

Whole Foods' customers are health-conscious, offers you an annual physical. If you hit a target heart rate and cholesterol level, Blue Shield (whose financial risk is lowered) rewards you with a $100 deposit into a SmartyPig savings account. For every dollar that you save in SmartyPig, you get half-price deals with four hundred other companies in their Mesh network.

As a member of this Mesh "ecosystem" you are: (1) eating healthy food; (2) getting in a little exercise walking to the car-share garage; (3) congratulating yourself on lowering your cho-lesterol and your carbon footprint; and (4) collecting a bonus from your health insurance and getting money in your bank account, which you can leverage for discounts at businesses whose offers are specifically tailored to you. Maybe a deal on a family ski vacation in Aspen? Your four-door hybrid—with tire chains in the trunk and a (shared) Thule ski rack on top—is waiting.

2

The Mesh Advantage

WHAT'S HERE: network power, leveraged; panning for gold, or meet my friend, the filter; spice up your mesh with partners.

Wayne Huizenga was in waste management before he started Blockbuster. I met him years ago when I was at AOL, and I said to him, "Wow, you must be really into entertainment and film."

"Eh, I don't give a crap about that stuff," he said. We were in a high-rise building in downtown Manhattan.

"You know what I care about?" he said. "Look out that window. It's a beautiful site, isn't it?"

I looked out the window. "All I see down there are Dumpsters," I said.

"That's what I mean! I'm all about renting," he said. "I buy it once, and wherever it moves, I keep making money on my old investment."

Wayne is a serial entrepreneur. All of his businesses, from trash to movies, revolve around the same theme—buying something once and renting it many times. Wayne understands: when you sell to own, there's only one major transaction. That's the ownership model.

Like Wayne's businesses, the Mesh model is based on a series of transactions, on sharing something over and over. Creating a share platform is the first, necessary-but-not-sufficient building block of the Mesh. The second is to create an information infrastructure that takes advantage of mobile, Web, and social networks. Then each interaction, and transaction, becomes an opportunity to gather and exchange information with a customer. (Blockbuster, as we shall see, failed to implement this critical second feature of the Mesh, at great cost to the company.)

Good Mesh businesses are smart about combining more frequent customer contact with enhanced information sources to create and refine superior experiences, partnerships, products, and offers. That, in short, is the Mesh advantage. This chapter explores that advantage in depth and paints a picture of an altogether new and different business landscape made possible by the Mesh.

the value of data is in its transformation.

Every Mesh transaction is an opportunity to deliver on the promise you make to your customers—to give them convenient access to customized goods and services. And every time you deliver on your promise, you create a greater bond of trust with the people, communities, partners, or markets you are serving. That in turn creates more opportunities to collect useful information from them, which helps you further tailor and personalize your offering. This dynamic is now common on the Web. Expedia knows you're going to New York and offers discount tickets on

Broadway. Kayak, Travelocity, iTunes, Lovefilm, Netflix, Amazon, Chegg, Barneys, and many others make customized offerings designed to improve over time. As the timing and relevance of the offers improve, so does consumer satisfaction and trust in the brand. Greater trust translates into recommendations through your customers' social networks, expanding your reach. Customers become more receptive to additional offerings from your company, or from your trusted partners, who in turn can help you expand your market. Call it a "virtuous circle of trust": Learn. Test. Play. Engage. Then rinse and repeat.

Just on the basis of the number of transactions that occur, Mesh businesses are in much better position to be an everyday part of their customers' lives. If I own a bike shop, I typically only have a short time to interact with a customer around the purchase of the bike, and may not see that person again for years, if ever. If I'm running a bike-sharing service, the number of transactions during those years will be many times greater. Each transaction is an occasion to put my brand in front of the customer. The increased interaction allows me to glean more information, to improve service, and to make timely, relevant personal offers. I can offer different bikes for different occasions, or for various members of the family and visitors. I can enable the customer to choose a favorite bike remotely, and offer repeat customers heavy discounts during low-use periods. I understand better how to address a family's needs—and how to enrich their life experiences. Simply put, your business is first in line to amaze your customers, to win again and again. In some instances, new gear will come on the market, and people may be unsure about spending money on it just yet. When a Mesh offering is added to an existing product sales model, new customers can try before they buy. They become early purchasers and enthusiasts of new product lines for your market.

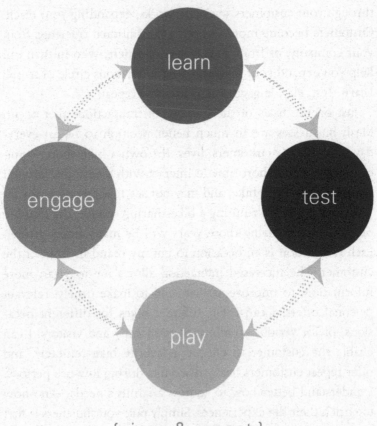

virtuous cycle of trust

learn

test

engage

play

{ rinse & repeat }

Build Trust. Grow Base. Refine Offers.

That's the kind of leverage a Mesh model uses to expand traditional repertoires.

The virtuous circle of trust enables you, as the business owner, to rapidly and frequently interact with customers and prospects, and their friends and families. You learn more about what services or products they want and how to deliver them. Bike sharing, for example, has become one of the fastest growing forms of transportation, especially in Europe. But in the initial offerings, problems emerged. A common one is that customers often want to pick the bike up in one location and return it to another, which presents a logistical challenge to the service. In Paris, which has one of the most advanced bike-sharing programs, users often left the bike at the bottom of a hill, so they wouldn't have to pedal up. Solutions include having people pay a premium for dropping the bike in a different location or adding a small motor that helps them power the bike up a hill. Paris is testing solutions with groups of users—and like a good Mesh enterprise, they are also sharing their results with bike-sharing services in other cities.

In the case of the clothing exchange company thredUP, the owners revised their core offering—they started out focusing solely on men's shirts—after repeated interactions with their customers revealed a greater opportunity in exchanging kids' clothes. They revamped their home page to focus entirely on children's clothing—a move they learned by listening to data and feedback from their customers.

A new San Francisco chocolate company, TCHO, takes a novel approach to engaging with, and learning from, its customers. TCHO produces "beta editions" of its dark chocolate. Based on customer feedback and continuous flavor development, new versions of the chocolate emerge as often as every thirty-six hours. Version 1.0 went through 1,026 iterations in a year.

thredUP

One November morning in 2008, James Reinhart stood in front of his full closet, but couldn't find a thing to wear. His predicament sparked an idea: What if he could find a guy his size willing to swap shirts? Consignment and secondhand clothing stores are fine, James thought, but they aren't convenient for busy people who want to swap clothes. Driven by the desire to create an efficient and convenient clothing exchange, James and his cofounders Oliver Lubin and Chris Homer started thredUP, the Internet-enabled clothing exchange platform. Its concept: "out with the old-to-you, in with the new-to-you."

Initially, the company imagined using price points to facilitate swaps. But what a headache: How would thredUP accurately determine a shirt's value? It became clear that using basic measurables—such as brand, size, and condition—would help thredUP arrange shirt-for-shirt swaps. So in early 2009, two hundred men in seventeen states were invited to exchange long-sleeved, button-down shirts. It was a smash.

Within a year of launching, thredUP's membership exploded to 9,000. Men and women exchanged shirts and blouses after signing up for a free membership. Members list clothing items they want to swap and items they want to receive in their "exchange closet." ThredUP then sells mailers to use in the exchange (the first two cost $5 total, and subsequent groups of three cost $25). When members send the mailer with their clothes to thredUP, the company validates the clothing's quality and promptly sends clothes of equal value in return.

ThredUP members were pleased with the transactions—80 percent satisfied that what they received was better than what they gave away—but soon alerted the company to a bigger niche: children's clothing. The founders, who are customers themselves and deep listeners, have followed the suggestion. The company has now shifted to a focus on kids. Clearly, children are on a growth plan—every six months or so they need a whole new wardrobe!

Members enjoy getting a package in the mail with "new" clothes. It arrives and feels like a gift; you know it's for you, but you're not exactly sure what awaits.

If you're wondering whether your wardrobe is ripe for an exchange, take thredUP's nifty questionnaire to figure out just how much money the clothes you're *not* using are worth. ThredUP uses an algorithm to calculate how many articles of clothing you might have to swap, the dollar value, and how much money you might spend at thredUP to refresh your closet.

For taste testing, the owners devised a flavor wheel consisting of what they call the inherent flavors in cacao: chocolaty, fruity, nutty, floral, earthy, and citrus. Since TCHO somewhat fanatically manages the sources, harvesting, and manufacturing of its own chocolate, the company can respond quickly to customer taste tests. Businesses like TCHO and thredUP continually ask: Are there other services or products you'd like us to provide? Are there other brands that you're keen on? How else can we make your life simpler, less costly, and more enjoyable?

from the digital to the physical.

Every day, more parts of the physical world join data networks. Increasingly, usage and location information from multiple sources—including embedded chips, mobile GPS, RFID tracking of goods, and UPC codes—can be fused with data collected from the Web to create digital portraits of customer preferences, including what brands they trust. Adding location data is a critical step. The new networks do not manage only strictly digital products, such as e-books; they can now connect you to physical products and services, like a hot meal (which to date can only be digitalized on *Star Trek*).

OpenTable, for example, is a restaurant reservation system with a mobile phone app. Say you're leaving a movie downtown. The mobile phone app will locate where you are standing and map nearby restaurants with available tables. You can look over the menu and reviews, get directions, and make a reservation while you're headed toward the restaurant. The mobile network locates and connects you in time and space with a physical place, the restaurant. The social network, in the form of online reviews by other diners and friends, informs your choice. If you text a note to the restaurant, you might find a physical product—perhaps a dish of spicy Szechuan noodles—hot and waiting when you arrive. Meanwhile, OpenTable and its network of restaurants learn over time, particularly if you send in reviews, which restaurants you, or people like you, prefer. They collect information that allows them to make more relevant and timely offers in the future, customized for you. It's a bit like having a personal concierge living in your phone who knows your favorite table and drink. For restaurants, the system improves their ability to predict traffic and inventory, which makes operations more efficient, and helps fill tables by offering time-specific promotions.

Similarly, Volkswagen recently launched the "App My Ride" contest, soliciting ideas for a future VW infotainment system involving mobile phone apps. The automaker has suggested app categories ranging from eco-mobility to networking and communication, and from games to travel utility. Contributors might design apps that facilitate car-to-car communication or allow drivers to book specific, location-based travel activities. Soon, with a quick tap of your finger, you will be able to leverage network data and connect to physical goods and services on the go. Volkswagen is opening a door to a "car as platform" model, in which third-party developers create a rich ecosystem of apps to customize and extend the lifetime use of an automobile. It is early, but this approach promises to create substantial value for businesses and buyers alike.

We're in a new stage in the information revolution. All the information coming together, whether it's personal to me, or specific to women who share certain characteristics or behaviors with me, allows a company to make me irresistible, timely, and customized offers. The challenge to a Mesh entrepreneur is to leverage an infrastructure optimized for real-customer personalization. Successful Mesh businesses harness information from customers, combine it with data from physical products and social networks, and then use that information to satisfy customers, and their friends, in ways never before dreamed of.

network power, leveraged.

Indeed, this new stage of the information revolution favors the Mesh. The story of Web-based commerce is one of learning how to make information more detailed and valuable. The first wave of Internet companies focused on sharing information between parties—in the most basic case, selling an e-mail service. As companies aggregated digital information, they began to realize its value. The information allowed them to target customers and tailor offers of digital products. Yahoo! hosted a free e-mail service because it gave the company an easy way to identify and offer users other digital products, such as Yahoo! Photos. The user's personal information converted her from an anonymous browser hit to a specific individual with an e-mail address. The conversion increased the value of the company's advertising business, and enabled Yahoo! to offer additional Web-hosted services under the same registration system and user name.

Internet companies then figured out ways of making money by selling specific information to third parties. Google, for example, sells search terms—the term "deadbolt" might be sold to an online hardware store that offers locks. In the next wave, Web 2.0, social networking empowered customers to become more active in shaping products and services. Yelp, for example, only functions because millions of people rate and comment on their experiences with businesses. The conversation is two-way, which makes the information more valuable. The customer is also more deeply engaged, and more likely to use their social networks to recommend products and services.

Web 2.0 has changed the relationship between customers and companies in multiple ways. For one, customers can make or break certain products and services through recommendations, requests, or complaints. They are also more powerful in shaping what products and services companies offer, and how these are upgraded. As that new power converges with mobility and real-time location data, something transformative is being born. Successful companies will increasingly participate directly with customers and prospective customers to design and refine their products and services, tailored to the individual, and delivered where and when the person wants them.

In their new book *The Power of Pull*, John Hagel, John Seely Brown, and Lang Davison argue that companies will decisively shift away from pushing stocks of inventory on customers. Instead, businesses will make goods and services available to customers in the place, time, and manner that they want. The company doesn't push; the customer pulls. Here, too, access beats ownership.

Mesh businesses are ahead of that curve. They are using what we've collectively learned about what works in a Web business for *digital* products and applying it to the sharing of *physical* products. This is the next phase. The mobile Web helps users locate a product to share, or people to share with. In most cases, a person actually has to get up from her chair to participate—it's a physical experience, not just a virtual one. By linking the Web, mobile technology, and physical venues and products, the relevant offers can be located in a specific place and time. Just as someone uses the OpenTable app to make a last-minute restaurant reservation on a mobile phone, he can make a date with a bike, tool, or car.

their billions. our inheritance. or, who's that standing on my shoulders?

Mesh businesses also begin with a huge technical advantage. The billions spent in developing the Internet, mobile infrastructure, and certain large platforms—such as Amazon, Google, 3G, Facebook, PayPal, and eBay—have lowered the financial and time barriers for starting new businesses. This key development in the evolution of the Internet favors Mesh businesses. From product development to marketing, Mesh businesses can and do deploy assets they don't own but can easily access. Ebay, for example, pioneered a Mesh-style global platform that enables people to sell almost anything. Other available assets include cloud computing services, social networks, and national postal services, UPS, and FedEx package services. Leveraging existing, well-established, scaled, and trusted assets significantly lowers the cost and risk of starting a new enterprise.

This is a big reason that Mesh businesses are starting to thrive. The enhanced ability to leverage existing platforms, and lower incremental costs, is a big reason that Mesh businesses are starting to thrive. If we were to start Ofoto today, offering the same products and services (reliable network storage, customer order systems, backend systems, printing and shipping facilities), I estimate that it would take 10 percent of the nearly $60 million we raised at the time. Why? The cloud computing networks, tools, talent pool, and software as a service (SaaS) vendors in place today would allow us to go to market faster with far less capital. That reality improves nearly every aspect of getting a venture successfully off the ground and in condition to grow— the number of core staff required, the funding needed, and the time it takes to get to market.

the seriously friendly effect.

Knowing how to take advantage of social networks is important to Mesh businesses. Say you connect to 10,000 people who have more than 200 friends on Facebook or orkut. And imagine you impress those people with the quality of your service. Some number of them will share information about your business with their friends and family on their social networking sites. Or one will just mention it over coffee. That's leverage.

At Ofoto, we encouraged the sharing of digital photos among social networks of friends and family. We knew that people enjoyed sharing photos of events, and shaped our offer accordingly. At the time, people would share photo albums with on average five or six of their friends and family. Someone would go to a party, take a bunch of pictures, and share them. Friends and family members would see how fabulous they looked in a photo, and then buy the print, often signing up for an account of their own. We would pay to acquire one customer and get five for free. The "network effect," as it's known, was a new phenomenon then, but has grown dramatically in the years since. Newer photo services, such as Olapic, allow shots from anyone who attends an event, such as a wedding, to be uploaded in a single place and shared on social networking sites.

panning for gold. or meet my friend, the filter.

In social networks, certain people act as "discoverers." I am one in particular domains. My friends expect me to occasionally find new music, or artists, or great restaurants and bars, or relatively unknown spots in faraway places. Likewise, in my life I have discoverers who influence my choices in certain arenas. If one tells me to read a book, check out a new musician, try a restaurant, or see a film, I'm likely to do it. (Of course, there are also those friends whose recommendations go in the "ignore" bin.) A discoverer might have five hundred or more friends on Facebook or followers on Twitter. If he has influence with half of those friends and followers, that's real leverage for any Mesh business. A recent study by McKinsey concluded that a recommendation from a "trusted source" like a friend or family member was fifty times more likely to persuade someone to buy a product or try a new brand.

The same study reported that word of mouth is the "primary factor" behind between 20 and 50 percent of purchases, and emphasized the expanded role of information networks in driving this development. Further, marketing campaigns based on "considerable" word of mouth turn out to be more effective than traditional advertising.

We're in the midst of a social phenomenon at takeoff. When someone shares his experience of using RedesignMe, UpMyStreet, MOG, BigCarrot, or ParkingCarma on Facebook, Bebo, or Twitter, he educates the friends and colleagues who are following him. And they are far more likely to trust what he says over what the company says about itself. This is the "curator effect," a term coined by marketing expert Steven Addis. The phenomenon represents an enormous change from the days when companies could carefully protect their brands, confident that people were getting their information from three TV networks. As Addis writes, "It's not your consumer power that terrifies marketers. It's your sway over millions of other consumers as a curator. A curator with unlimited resources to research products, review them for others, and expose the disingenuous. A curator with the ability to transmit on a mass scale. And a curator with credibility corporations have all but squandered."

Kickstarter, a new platform for micro-funding new arts projects, is self-consciously taking advantage of social networks and the curator effect to expand its business. It has made an explicit effort to invite artists who are influential and have a following to participate on its site.

very meshy. very cool.

People who support new artists on Kickstarter or make wine with Crushpad feel that they are smarter and lighter, at the forefront of a new wave. They feel cool. That's a big part of being Mesh happy. The Mesh businesses and a Mesh lifestyle are aspirational. People will feel drawn to the Mesh the same way they once felt compelled to buy an MP3 player, a mobile phone, or an SUV. They will Mesh their lives by simplifying them, reducing their stress. Using the Mesh will confer status. Meshy is going to be good.

Customers will like saving money and feeling richer, through reducing the costs associated with owning things. But the Mesh sharing experience can also make people feel wealthy in other ways. Throughout the world, there is a palpable hunger for a greater sense of community. I was fascinated by one project that an educational charity group called the Eden Project launched in July 2009 throughout the U.K. They called it "The Big Lunch." Nearly a million people came out, put a table in front of their home, brought out some food, and had lunch with their neighbors on the streets. I saw it in stories, photos, and videos of the event that were uploaded on Flickr, YouTube, and other sites. It was wonderful to witness. I was struck that the British, who are not known to be the most outwardly effusive group on the planet, felt that they wanted to reinspire community in this wide-reaching way.

Mesh businesses, because they generate more information

Kickstarter

In April 2009, a new way to fund creative ideas and projects made a splash on the Internet. Designers, filmmakers, journalists, inventors, artists, and other creatives flocked to Kickstarter, a platform for soliciting small yet consequential monetary contributions from donors. Kickstarter is powered by a unique funding method that is *not* about personal investing: project creators maintain 100 percent ownership of their intellectual property.

Starting a project on Kickstarter is free, but currently projects are posted by invitation only, and must be based in the United States. Founder Perry Chen says Kickstarter plans to assist international project creators in the future. To initiate a project, creators set a funding goal and a deadline of up to ninety days after the project's posting date. Kickstarter offers advice to help creators meet their funding goal on time and to attract possible investors with compelling project descriptions and clever rewards to funders. Gifts have been as simple as a pen boasting the project's name for a $5 donation, and as elaborate as a hot-air balloon ride for a donation of $150.

After "micro-patrons" make donations, they receive updates on the project's funding progress. If donors become invested in a project's success, they can send e-mails to the creator, link the project proposal to their Facebook pages, or Tweet about it to raise awareness of

the project and help get funding. With viral support, donations can pile up quickly: one $8,900 book project was 200
percent funded within the first forty-eight hours. Even if
the funding goal is surpassed, projects can accept pledges
until the funding deadline arrives. Kickstarter applies a fee
of 5 percent to the amount raised. The caveat: if a funding goal isn't achieved, all pledges are canceled, and no
money changes hands.

As donors and artists bring their own social networks
to the site, the potential for donors to find new interesting
projects, and for artists to reach more donors, naturally
builds. Perry reports that Kickstarter is increasing the number of projects and the volume of its transactions at a rate
of about 20 percent a month. Kickstarter has momentum, a
growing following, angel investors, and a big idea—perfect
ingredients for success in the Mesh. A similar service is off
and running in France called Kisskissbankbank.

and contact with communities, can help provide these rich social experiences. In the Mesh, opportunities abound to rub up against an eye-opening idea that inspires new thinking about the quality of life or work. For Mesh businesses, it is an ongoing imperative to understand the community, what its members consider valuable, and how to deliver that value. If you do, they'll love you for it. And think you're cool, too.

3

Mesh Design

WHAT'S HERE: heirloom design, or the
half-life of crap; the welcome return of
Mr./Ms. Fixit; design is continuous and
two-way; impersonate nature wherever
possible.

When my friend Joaquina first arrived in the United States
from Chile, and her camera, or bike, or shoes developed a problem, she'd ask where to take them to be fixed. People would look
at her as if she was from another planet. "Fixed?" she heard.
"No, no, it's just cheaper to throw it away and get a new one."
I hear people say it all the time. I've said it. But that sentence
should make all the hairs on the back of our necks stand up.
As the architect William McDonough has quipped, "Where is
away?"

The mantra of the ownership business model is simply: "Sell
more." Taken to the extreme, this mantra has severely warped
the basic principles of good design. Standing before the Egyptian
pyramids, one marvels at the beauty of their design, but also that
they have endured for thousands of years. At Sacsayhuamán, in

earthquake-prone Cuzco, Peru, engineers struggle to understand how the Incans built an outdoor arena of irregular boulders, some weighing hundreds of tons, that even today fit together so snugly that you can barely slide a credit card between them. Architectural students study the churches and temples of Europe and Asia to absorb the underlying principles. The buildings awe us with their beauty, while retaining their structural integrity for centuries. For most of human history, those who designed the tools and temples, the roads and aqueducts, the musical instruments and microscopic lenses, have sought to make products and structures that are durable, functional, efficient, and attractive.

Somewhere we got off track. Today's industrial designers do make artful objects. But even the most elegant HDTV or laptop computer or ballpoint pen is built with the expectation that it will soon become obsolete or disposable, so that a new one can be sold. Contractors build new homes with flimsy materials that reduce the initial building cost, but drive up the longer-term maintenance, energy, and environmental costs.

The arrival of the Mesh signals a new dynamic in design, and a return to first principles. Successful participation in the Mesh requires a product that holds up to repeated uses. One that is highly functional, fun, and easy to use. One designed to be repaired, upgraded, and "upcycled" at the end of its life. This dynamic had already found traction in so-called green design and the gradual reform of economic and policy incentives that encourage obsolescence and waste. The Mesh will deepen and accelerate this trend toward design that is more durable, functional, and adaptable, as well as more profitable.

In a Mesh business, products are shared. The flow of information about the products, including feedback from customers, is constant. As a result, favored products are built to last and keep functioning, adapt to different users, and be capable of repair and upgrading. The logic of the throwaway culture is completely reversed. Mesh design is:

Durable. Products that many people use must be safe, well built, and longer lasting.

Flexible. Products accommodate different users with design that is modular, but easily personalized.

Reparable. Standardized parts and transparent design allow products to be fixed and reused, rather than trashed, encouraging a culture of repair and reuse.

Sustainable. Design that reduces natural resource destruction and waste, which is ever more expensive, improves efficiency and reduces overall costs.

heirloom design. or the half-life of crap.

For years now, the common folklore in the West has been that the cheapest way to replace many appliances is to throw the old one away and buy a new one. "Planned obsolescence"—products designed with the expectation that they will have a short life and be replaced—has ruled the day. In contrast, the Mesh motivates designers to create timeless products that can be used over and over again. Saul Griffith, a respected physicist and inventor and a friend, has coined a name for this built-to-last practice: "heirloom design." Heirloom design is something that's built to endure for generations. The virtue is baked into the fundamental thought process.

Heirloom products favor retooling, repairing, upgrading, or

recycling. MontBlanc pens, Volvos and BMWs, Craftsman and Victorian homes, Eames furniture, vintage clothing made from natural fibers—all are products and styles made from the best materials available at the time. Well-designed products like these hold or increase their value over a long time. They are prized sufficiently to warrant and sustain repair services.

The problem, of course, is the price. People don't resist buying a Rolex watch because they don't like it. For the average person, a Rolex is an absurd acquisition because it costs thousands of dollars. But for the sake of efficiency—and the environment—it would be better for everybody to buy a more durable (and consequently more expensive) watch, car, home furnace, MP3 player, and mobile phone. In the Mesh, an individual doesn't have to foot the cost of an heirloom design product alone. The cost of shared goods is spread over many transactions and people, so the quality can often be higher compared to products an individual customer could afford to own outright. Better-designed products also count as a competitive advantage for a Mesh business.

Durable, well-designed products are usually safer products because they are less likely to break or fail. Mesh businesses have strong incentives, including maintaining their customers' trust, to buy safe products and to keep them in good repair. Because they buy in bulk, and collect actionable information from people and products, they are likely to know which products are durable and safe. Mesh businesses are also in a better position to anticipate and assess potential safety problems, and address them when they occur. The availability of training and concierge services, for example, makes using products such as power tools safer. The ease and speed of communication with a Mesh service, through mobile devices and the Web, means there's always someone to call. If something breaks or stalls, the business is often in a position to know instantly via chips embedded in the product itself. In some cases, a company representative may be able to diagnose and remedy the problem remotely.

just for you.

As I've discussed previously, a key advantage for Mesh businesses is the use of rich information to personalize products and services. There are several ways to achieve this. Products can be designed to adjust easily for different users, but in a way that is not time-consuming or expensive, and doesn't compromise the product's primary functionality. One of my personal favorites is a kid's bike that expands or contracts in size to fit the rider. Just in case the kid grows.

If a product design is modular, different modules can be added to or subtracted from the basic structure. That can be as simple as adding a luggage rack to the car, or carrying a variety of blades for a circular saw. And mobile devices will offer users the continually expanding ability to personalize products and services. A phone app could be programmed to automatically adjust the bike seat and handlebars to your preferences. Another could quickly locate jeans to your taste and size in a clothes-sharing service. The wireless connection that opens your shared car might also adjust the seat, temperature settings, and radio station presets to your liking, while pulling up your frequent destinations for the GPS.

Another type of personalization is simply to offer a range of options. For instance, I would like to see more companies offer cargo bikes, which have a longer chassis. On a cargo bike, a parent can carry a kid or two to the market with no crying—by the parent or child—and no lost beverages. Most car trips are for less than two miles from home. A bike becomes a more realistic form of transportation when you can use it to haul a small piece of furniture, or carry three bags of groceries and a child back and forth to a store a few miles away. In North America only a few companies, such as Specialized and Trek with Gary Fisher, make or distribute cargo bikes. In Denmark and in Amsterdam, a number of companies build cargo bikes.

The cargo bike example highlights a key advantage to Mesh businesses. They often offer different tools for different jobs—a cargo bike for trips to the store, but a light, fast road bike for taking a ride around the park. Having access to a variety of tools, such as electric routers or hydraulic lifts, is cumbersome under the ownership model. But it makes sense for a tool library. A man in Sonoma County, California, created just such a library by asking people to donate tools they weren't using, and then lending the tools out. With a car-sharing service, you might check out a van to take a group to the park on Saturday, a pickup truck to haul lumber on Sunday, and a small hybrid to drive to work on Monday. It's all about having access to the right tool for the right job.

fix it, the sequel.

The repair shops that used to dot U.S. neighborhoods—for shoes, bikes, clothes, vacuum cleaners, electronics, cars, and small appliances—have largely been pushed aside by cheap throwaway goods. As Mesh businesses acquire or employ physical goods that are more long-lasting, the incentives are also likely to shift back toward repairing things.

Since the constituent parts of a product typically deteriorate at different rates, standardized parts are more easily reused, replaced, and recycled. Modular design is served by a degree of standardization. If many of the parts of different bicycles are interchangeable, for example, it becomes easy to salvage parts from a broken bike. The Mesh generally encourages open and agreed-upon design standards. Standards, even as they evolve and improve over time, make it easier to coordinate offerings with business partners. Standards make it easier to share information across platforms, as well as lowering the cost of making offers across several platforms.

While Mesh businesses are well positioned to offer specialized tools, they also promote standardization of certain platforms and components. Standardization of screws, nuts, and bolts was essential for advancing construction, auto manufacturing, and any number of other industries. The same goes for street and sidewalk specs, as well as for less concrete items such as ISBN numbers as a categorization system for books. The Web itself relies on standard protocols, and has thrived for that reason. Without industry-wide cooperation or government regulation, companies have traditionally vied to set and control standards and formats to monopolize their category. Unfortunately, what may be in the short-term interest of one company can hold back development of entire industries, and confuse customers. For example, as I write, Apple is being criticized for failing to include Adobe Flash capability on the new iPad. Some colorful comments have been exchanged. Apple, which has historically been proprietary about its own software, would like to force the adoption of a different protocol. Perhaps the iPad will, as Apple argues, offer a better multimedia platform than Flash. In the meantime, customers are left with less-than-satisfactory options.

sustain this. welcome your product home.

An early version of heirloom design, "sustainable design," is already hot in the best schools. Coauthors Michael Braungart and William McDonough propose in the book Cradle to Cradle that all products need to be designed so they may be reused or later reclaimed. The base materials themselves are shared, which is why they must not be toxic. Their proposal would significantly reduce waste and encourage designers and manufacturers to choose materials deliberately and holistically. Cradle to Cradle relies on the understanding that there is no possibility of throwing something away without consequences to soil and groundwater.

The next stage of product design is less about creating new, "greener" stuff and more about building durable products that can be shared. Designers should imitate nature by using structures and materials that endure. Of course, the most durable shared bike, car, watch, or other product does have a finite life cycle, even if it is well maintained. The goal is to start with good quality, conserve the core materials, and preserve the virtues of the product as it goes through its life cycle.

Earth is the ultimate share platform. Thoughtful product design conserves nature by reducing the carbon footprint and lowering waste. As citizens on the planet, as well as entrepreneurs in Mesh businesses, we should all want this. Reducing waste is also called operating efficiently. In fact, for economic reasons alone, all businesses should aspire to reduce waste. DuPont, for example, saved over $2 billion by reducing its emissions by 70 percent between 1990 and 2004. Successful Mesh enterprises strive to equal the convenience of the ownership model while trimming out the extra fat, environmentally and financially. (Some also trim the waist. Just walking three blocks each way for a shared car, instead of out to the garage, can make a difference.)

The Europeans have made progress in avoiding disposable products. Many governments in Europe require manufacturers to take back their products when they are no longer useful, creating a powerful incentive to employ cradle-to-cradle strategies. Companies then upcycle the parts and materials into new products. Although some of these practices are being adopted in the United States—many states now have requirements for manufacturers to recycle or upcycle electronic products—tax dollars still subsidize waste by paying for landfills and price supports to oil corporations.

design is continuous and two-way.

Since Mesh businesses are in closer touch, their customers' priorities, desires, and complaints float more quickly to the top than in traditional businesses. Collected data can be fed back to the manufacturer to improve the product over time. This is important because, for many products, manufacturers and designers have become separated from the ultimate user. The retail distribution channel creates a chasm that prevents customer feedback from reaching the designers in a timely way and without filters. For a car manufacturer with new releases targeted, say, to parents or to first-time drivers, a car-sharing company is a treasure chest of new information. The manufacturer might also survey groups of members for feedback: What did you like or dislike about the car? Was it easy to find things? Did you find the back seat comfortable? Did your mobile phone, GPS, or music device pop in simply and function well? What would you change about the car? This is the Mesh "virtuous circle of trust" in action: Learn. Test. Play. Engage. Rinse and repeat.

Currently, the long cycle time to design and manufacture a car is absurd. Better, more timely information from customers may speed it up. To close this gap, a few companies have formed that facilitate direct feedback between customers and manufacturers, including feedback 2.0 in France and Get Satisfaction in the States. Other sites, such as the U.K.'s FixMyStreet, perform a similar function for local governments, allowing easy feedback from citizens about neighborhood problems.

think far. build near.

The Mesh is poised to inspire a whole new generation of heirloom designers who will in turn fuel and support Mesh business strategies. A German site, Open Design, uses the methods of open software design, with creative commons licenses, and applies them to furniture and other products. Another site, RedesignMe, is a platform for companies seeking design solutions and designers offering them. The good ones are adopted and paid for. We're at the beginning of a new era of design that uses the Web, customer engagement, and buckets of imagination to create better goods and services.

4

In with the Mesh

WHAT'S HERE: why now?; what gets measured gets managed; hidden assets in what some call waste; being dense is cool; the value of your customers' footsteps, or how can I make you never go?

Giant corporations cultivate an air of permanence and inevitability. They want you to think the big brands of yesterday will be just as strong forever. Economic historians know better. In eras of great instability—and the financial crisis that broke out in 2008 is one whopper of an upheaval—pillar companies crumble. New ones rise up. Few who begin the crisis on top come out on top. Who would have believed a few years ago that Merrill Lynch, whose muscular bronze bull long served as the symbol of the strength and power of Wall Street, would be liquidated for pennies on the dollar?

According to a recent study by the Kauffman Foundation, nearly half of the companies on *Inc.* magazine's 2008 list of fastest-growing companies were founded in a recession or bear market. Fifty-seven percent of the Fortune 500 companies were founded during downturns, an above-average number of them during the Great Depression. Instability forces change.

In fact, many of the biggest brands in the world today are vulnerable. Most people simply don't trust them. It's tough to get 96 percent of Americans to agree on anything. But according to a 2009 Harris poll, that's the number that agree Wall Street and credit card companies are dishonest and can't be trusted. Only 14 percent now trust big business, period.

The recession has changed people's attitudes in other ways as well. According to one study, eight out of ten Americans are "inclined to buy less stuff," and nine out of ten are considering "opting for a simpler life." This questioning helps explain why popular books on thrift, such as Theodore Malloch's *Thrift: Rebirth of a Forgotten Virtue* and Ronald Wilcox's *Whatever Happened to Thrift?* (reissued in 2010), are turning up in bookstores. The economic crisis has shaken our values and forced us to reconsider what's important.

reflection, triage, and a two-car garage.

At a recent TED (Technology, Entertainment, Design) conference, I saw a Greek friend of mine whose family still lives in Greece. He is now a wealthy venture capitalist living in northern California, and spends almost no time in his home country. His family, he said, thinks he's a mental case. With all of his wealth, why does he continue to work crazy hours far away from the people who love him? We laughed about it, but our conversation caused me to think: What if we've sold ourselves a very large but fundamentally wrong story? When stuff became cheap, and then credit became cheap, we filled our lives with stuff—not the things we really care about. What if we're on this overcrowded little hamster wheel that won't get us to a happy place?

As I looked at my own life and listened to people around me, I realized that people were talking less about what they owned, and more about what mattered in their lives—things like their health, friendships, traveling, meeting new people, getting inspired, sharing good food, creating great memories, and having more time to spend with their families. I was also hearing: Hey, I don't need two cars. Maybe I don't need all these toys in my house. Maybe I don't even need this big house. They were beginning to wonder about the intense focus on "acquisition" in our culture over the last fifty years. When I traveled to Chile, Argentina, and several places in Europe—Copenhagen, Amsterdam, Paris, and Brussels—this conversation became more ubiquitous and substantially louder.

why now?

The current economic environment, in which people are reconsidering what they care about, holds rich promise for the Mesh. As in jokes, timing in business is essential. It's good not to be late, or too early. One might ask, "Why the Mesh, now?" Five disparate vectors make the Mesh particularly viable and rewarding within today's economic and cultural landscape:

1. The economic crisis has bred **distrust of old companies**.

2. The crisis has also encouraged people to **reconsider what's valuable** and important to them.

3. **Climate change** is forcing up the cost of doing business, including the making and selling of throwaway goods.

4. The growing population and greater urbanization create **densities** that favor Mesh businesses.

5. Information networks of all kinds have matured to the point where businesses can provide better and more personalized services exactly when needed.

a big dose of big brand distrust.

In Spanish, batir las claras is an expression that literally means "to beat egg whites into meringue." The phrase is used to imply that someone is just "puffing something up," making a lot of something from a little of nothing. The economic crisis exposed a whole host of untrustworthy characters that were "puffing up." Banks, insurance companies, brokerage houses, investors, and public companies were creating phony value. They deceptively highlighted the assets and hid the liabilities. Lehman Brothers, we now know, hid billions in losses through a deceptive accounting trick that top executives approved.

Citibank, AIG, Merrill Lynch, and Goldman Sachs took taxpayer TARP money and then paid themselves huge bonuses. People were justly infuriated. The executives defended the indefensible by declaring that the bonuses were in their contracts. (I've done plenty of contracts. Contracts can always be renegotiated.) Their actions deepened the chasm between individuals and big brands: the greater the chasm, the greater the resentment and distrust.

Older executives often know that their business model and brand are fading and squeeze the last juice from the fruit for themselves. Many of them grabbed what they could on the way out, leaving the rest of us mired in an economic maelstrom. A

Harvard study showed that the top five executives at Lehman Brothers and Bear Stearns cashed out equity and bonuses worth an average of $250 million each in the years leading up to their collapse. Executives at McDonald's, the U.S.-based airline companies (with the exception of JetBlue and Southwest), many of the utility companies, including AT&T, Verizon, and Comcast, and all the car companies have made similar moves to cash out early and often. When the principal shareholders are principal executives, and shareholders take precedence over everything else, corporate behavior is distorted. Conflicts of interests twist incentives, principles, and, inevitably, performance. That distortion has produced a deep distrust and fermented the I'm-mad-as-hell-and-I'm-not-going-to-take-it-anymore mood in much of the United States.

This distrust of old-model companies is fueling people's willingness to consider alternative business models, brands, and lifestyles. Nearly half of the people in the United States report that they are considering brands they hadn't earlier. They are more willing to try a community bank or car-sharing service. They will give a new merchant a second look because they have lost confidence in the brands they feel betrayed them. Plus, it's easier than ever to try new brands. New mobile Web services that connect people to local merchants and venues have been well received in European and U.S. markets. People appear keen to learn more about what local merchants can offer, and have responded well to promotional offers directed to their mobile phones from services like Gowalla, foursquare, Feest (in the Netherlands), MePlease, and Groupon.

Utilizing these new services as well as the pervasive reach of mobile phones, new ventures can create a "flash brand" that is finely tuned to a particular community at the right moment. Restaurant patrons, for example, might be invited to an impromptu tasting or live performance of a new band. Such flash brands provide chefs, investors, or sponsors with effective feedback while creating a sense of urgency among the desired audience. Using flash branding, a kind of "anti-restaurant" has even sprung up in the United Kingdom, United States, and Canada. Toronto recently hosted several new secret restaurants, like Charlie's Burgers, where you have to apply to be invited to a dining event at an unadvertised venue. Similar offerings unrelated to food will also be easier to design and deliver as social mobile services expand their reach and extend their capabilities. Flash brands are also an inexpensive and exciting way to test new brands and concepts. Merchants, artists, and others can even take a kind of "every fortnight" approach to doing business. By limiting the supply while generating an audience when and where it's needed, flash brands enable businesses to create a sense of uniqueness to the brand or offering.

There's also a generational transformation under way. Many older companies are pretty dumb about creating new products that will endear them to a younger generation. Some have gone to silly lengths—remember when Post had Barney Rubble don shades and do a 1980s rap to sell Fruity Pebbles cereal? In trying to be edgy, Pepsi stirred protests by suggesting ways the lonely single calorie in Pepsi Max might commit suicide.

This slow-footedness on the part of corporate behemoths— and the growing gulf between what brands stand for and the actual product desired or delivered—creates an opening for the Mesh. Hundreds of Mesh entrepreneurs have started companies in the past few years, providing alternatives to older brands. Although still a small part of the financial market, peer-to-peer lenders already compete with traditional banks for similar transactions, customer relationships, and capital. In the United States alone, Lending Club and Prosper have facilitated over $250 million in loans. Zopa, the first to do peer-to-peer lending, has expanded to Italy and Japan from its base in London. Smava offers similar services in Germany and plans to expand to other European markets. Other Mesh companies have found underserved financial niches. BigCarrot's platform matches lenders and business borrowers. SmartyPig creates incentives and premiums for customers to save, including discounted purchases with marketing partners. Mesh finance companies also specialize in other aspects of peer-to-peer transactions, including financing tuition, micro-lending, community-based financing, and more.

When older companies feel that Mesh businesses are threatening their core business, they will likely make a competing offering. Hertz and Avis could go into the bike-sharing business, offering the service at all the train stations in major cities. They have the infrastructure, capacity, and brand to do it. That doesn't mean that they'll take over the business overnight. As always, innovative companies will crack new markets. Other large companies may reason that if you can't beat 'em, join 'em. Some local banks, responding to the credit crisis, have partnered with peer-to-peer lending companies to offer customers loans or additional investment opportunities.

first things first.

The recession that started late in 2008 has pummeled individuals, towns, and businesses. Lost jobs and repossessed homes have forced families to move to new cities, move in with other family members, and change school districts. Over half of people in the United States and U.K. report that they personally know someone who lost his or her job. Innocent people who patiently built their careers had promotions blocked or were downsized (aka "made redundant"). Many were employed by apparently stable and well-trusted companies, such as Cadbury, Activision, Lufthansa, and Xerox. Although active, engaged, and productive all their lives, some people have been out of work over a year and are still looking. Others have watched their portfolio fall in value, forcing drastic reductions in their lifestyle or delaying their retirement indefinitely.

The trauma of the recession has forced many people to focus on what is really of value to them. The writer Po Bronson notes that a "crisis can actually take people from thinking about what's next to thinking about what is first." Many of us grew up with the aspiration to own our homes. We hoped that when we retired we would have a place to live without having to pay housing costs. In recent years, home equity was also a lucrative place to invest. As home prices increased, so too did the equity. But the continued recession, or "reset," as author Richard Florida calls it, has forced us to revisit childhood assumptions. Why is home ownership desirable? Does it ensure a less stressful, happier old age? Does the increased stress and high cost of buying, insuring, and maintaining a home for decades justify the anticipated stress reduction later in life? Perhaps we are moving into an era when feeling secure and happy will be uncoupled from what we individually own.

As the reality of the recession sank in, people began to question a lifestyle based on an unsatisfying job that required fancy clothes and a long commute. I know people who dissolved their businesses and reevaluated their careers. They thought about what made them happy, engaged, and excited. They imagined what work would be compelling, as well as economically viable. One friend, who had been in the tech business for a long time, couldn't get funding for her projects, despite a solid reputation. She eventually gave up her home and network of friends, changed professions, and courageously moved to the other side of the country to pursue a new opportunity.

Many people responded to the downturn by reevaluating their possessions—homes, cars, gear, and so on. Things they had worked so hard to acquire seemed to lose value. A survey by Kelton Research, under the heading "People's Mindsets Are Changing," reports that over half of Americans (56 percent) see the recession as an opportunity to live a less materialistic life. I know one woman who moved her family from San Francisco to Walla Walla, Washington. Before they left, she stored many of their possessions in nine of the "pods" that the storage companies use. A few months later, she called and asked me, "Do you remember what was in my house?" She said she couldn't really remember the stuff, and as far as she could tell, they'd already taken most everything they needed. She ended up moving only two of the nine pods to Walla Walla. Her recently cherished goods had turned into unnecessary clutter.

People are also more open to sharing. After all, sharing is not a brand-new idea. In the past, farmers were used to sharing things. There was an ethic of helping one another. Homes were often built together in the Amish style. More recently, many share platforms have thrived. As noted earlier, Conrad Hilton built a chain of international hotels that transformed the industry. Air travel took off. Energy cooperatives brought power to rural areas.

The big shift toward ownership arrived in the twentieth century, especially the second half. Government policy encouraged this trend by subsidizing gas and inexpensive home loans. The middle class drove to the suburbs and bought homes. Although pushed by public and corporate policy, people's desire for autonomy and convenience powered the trend. That desire sustained the large-scale movement toward ownership for half a century.

Autonomy was linked to status. Relying on your neighbors was out.

Today, perceptions are shifting again. The culture and psychology of ownership are in a transition—which isn't surprising. Cultural anthropologists have shown the transience of certain status indicators. Take the perception of beauty. Heavy people with porcelain white skin used to be considered beautiful. These features signaled wealth and time to devote to leisure. Now, beauty is connected to being svelte and tan, because that too tracks to leisure time. The constant is the relationship between beauty and leisure time. What's in today can be out tomorrow.

Currently, the fashion for what confers "the good life" is trending deeply toward the Mesh. From the 1950s through the '70s large cars were the fashion. When the gas crisis hit, more efficiency was in vogue until the SUV craze picked up steam. But huge cars and homes are again falling out of fashion. They are perceived as inefficient, wasteful, harmful, out of date, and unnecessary. It was a sign of the times when GM shut down the Hummer brand, due to bankruptcy. The fact is that if you're sitting right now with a whole lot of large single-family homes with four-car garages filled with SUVs, I'm going short on your stock.

In fact, recent studies, including one from the U.S. Department of Transportation, reveal early signs that the attitudes of youth toward car ownership and driving are shifting dramatically. The percentage of young people in the United States seeking a driver's license upon turning seventeen has been in rapid decline since 1998, and fell a third in the three decades between 1978 and 2008. Then, having a license was synonymous with adulthood and independence. Today, more young people are opting for car sharing, bike sharing, ride sharing, and mass transit for everyday personal transportation. Sustainable living is also trending up. Status formerly associated with autonomy and excess is now better achieved through civic behavior and community participation. When Brad Pitt helps build state-of-the-art green homes in the ravaged areas of New Orleans and Leonardo DiCaprio stumps for Global Green, they are reflecting the zeitgeist. A Zogby survey concluded that the virtues of simple living especially appeal to the 100-million-strong Millennial Generation, also called Gen Y. Zogby reports that this generation, ranging from those still in grade school to people in their twenties, is more socially conscious, environmentally aware, connected, and demanding as customers than earlier generations. Trendwatching.com reports they are accelerating a cultural shift toward sharing. Adolescent psychologist Michael Bradley told *USA Today* that young people want to avoid "being enslaved to the material goals they perceived their parents being caught up in."

There's also a growing realization that the true cost of something isn't necessarily what you paid at the register. Cars that guzzle gas and 5,000-square-foot homes that suck energy are losing resale value. In five years, the big house won't be competitive against a green home half the size, with solar and geothermal energy, and built of materials that increase heating and cooling efficiency. Companies such as Segway, Honda, Peugeot, Best Buy, and Toyota are all designing or market testing lightweight, low-carbon personal transport systems.

People are increasingly seeking a sustainable lifestyle. The standards have been changing for the past decade, and these changes are now accelerating, even in the United States. One indication of changing attitudes is the phenomenal growth of so-called green drivers of purchasing decisions. In a recent study by the Boston Consulting Group, fully 73 percent of consumers reported feeling it is important or very important that companies have a good environmental track record. In a poll of consumers in the United States, the United Kingdom, and Japan, respondents said they are placing more weight on "green" relative to other purchase drivers than they were before the recession, and that they will continue to do so when economic growth returns.

Of course, ownership won't become instantly passé. I'm not suggesting that people in the West will all sell their houses and live like monks. Nor should they. Most of us will want a personal computer, mobile phone, or new pair of jeans. But especially in many non-Western markets, people may skip the option of ownership in favor of convenient access to needed goods and services, just as they leapt over film to digital cameras and over landlines to mobile phones. There are already signs that some markets are primed to adopt Mesh models full-on and fast. For example, Singapore and Renault-Nissan have signed an agreement to make the city a testing ground for electric vehicles, or EVs. Singapore's size and density, and the commitment of its government, create the conditions in which EVs could replace fossil-fuel-burning vehicles. Singapore's commitment to innovation, including environmental and social projects, makes it a prime candidate for Meshing cars and other resources.

In the West, too, the widespread shift in values and perceptions has proved to be a boon for the Mesh. Like non-Mesh businesses, these new enterprises still need to serve customers and make a profit. The successful Mesh companies will be the ones that delight customers, grow trust in the brand and business itself, and make a profit.

the costs of climate change.

The throwaway economy contributes significantly to climate change. Landfills throw off methane gas, which accelerates global warming several times faster than carbon dioxide. Moving and disposing of waste requires energy. Power is required to sort and crush the trash and to refine one thing into something else. Energy, for the most part, is thermal, which generates greenhouse gases and pollutants.

For a very long time, the environmental liabilities of wasteful business practices have been hidden by government subsidies. Taxpayers have footed a lion's share of the bill for the environmental, health, and social costs of mining, clear-cutting, air pollution, and now climate change. Just as Lehman Brothers and Enron used accounting devices to hide the true picture of their finances, companies' environmental liabilities are often hidden. This is changing rapidly.

Within international business circles, there is growing recognition that company liability is often disguised by poor measurement, especially overreliance on the gross national product as a record of progress. In the words of Robert Kennedy Jr.:

> Our Gross National Product, now, is over eight hundred billion dollars a year, but that Gross National Product . . . counts air pollution and cigarette advertising, and ambulances to clear our highways of carnage. It counts special locks for our doors and the jails for those who break them. It counts the destruction of our redwoods and the loss of our natural wonder in chaotic sprawl.

Businesses already experience negative financial consequences from creating waste and pollution, as well as damage to their brands. Ceres, one of the monitors that posts the environmental balance sheet of publicly traded companies, exposes the buried liabilities that currently look like assets on the balance sheets of many industrial companies. It identifies five types of business risk related to climate change: regulatory, physical, reputational, competitive, and litigious.

◆ **Regulatory risk**—California and ten northeastern states already have enacted laws requiring emissions reductions. That trend is spreading quickly in the United States and the rest of the world.

◆ **Physical risk** comes from impacts such as extreme weather events.

◆ **Reputational risk** shows up in the way consumers research and make purchasing decisions based on "green" criteria. An increasing number of Web sites, such as GoodGuide, offer information on corporate behavior relative to climate change and other environmental and social criteria.

◆ **Competitive risks** are indicated by the growth of climate-friendly industries relative to those that aren't. For example, less than a quarter of American passenger cars and light-duty trucks meet emission standards in China, the fastest growing auto market in the world.

◆ **Litigious risk** is also expanding for polluting companies. Eight state attorneys are among the plaintiffs in a lawsuit against the five largest utilities for damages related to corporate contributions to climate change. The potential liability, the Ceres report says, is "immense."

The Deepwater Horizon catastrophe in the Gulf of Mexico offers an appalling example of how this liability puts all of us at extreme risk, not just the company involved. The oil company will pay untold billions in cleanup costs, and in settlements of public and private lawsuits. Their manipulation of regulations and regulators, misleading public reports, and suppression of scientific evidence will become the subject of media reports and government investigations for years to come. But the rest of us—especially the people and beings whose lives depended on that ecosystem's health—will pay most of the immense cost of the destruction to the region's flora and fauna and ocean and riparian ecosystems.

Companies like BP that make bad environmental choices about how their products are produced, distributed, used, and disposed of will gradually suffer increasingly negative financial consequences. The company's insurance costs, earnings per share, the subsequent profit paid to shareholders, and ultimately the brand equity will decline. (BP's much heralded "Beyond Petroleum" branding is a dead letter: Who will now trust them as an environmentally responsible company?) A bad record also affects investors' decisions. Two thirds of American investors report that they consider the ethics of a company before investing.

Then there's the consumer side. People are becoming increasingly conscious about where their food comes from, how they move around, and what products and brands they buy. And there are more ways to find out, including mobile apps such as Seafood Watch and GoodGuide, which allow you to evaluate a product's environmental record by scanning the UPC code. An MIT Web site called Sourcemap permits users to find out where products come from and what they are made of. This kind of information is guiding purchasing decisions. A 2008 study by Mintel, a leading market research company, reported that 36 percent of American adults claim to "regularly" buy green products—three times the number recorded sixteen months earlier. The number of people who "never" purchase green products had been cut in half.

As transparency about real costs—specifically, the cost of generating and managing waste—increases, environmentally responsible companies are more likely to be high performers financially. Some large corporations are already reaping the benefits of reducing greenhouse gas emissions. Walmart reports it will save an estimated $35–50 million for every one-mile-per-gallon efficiency gain in its truck fleet. The company has committed to increasing fuel efficiency by 25 percent. And General Electric has $50 billion worth of back orders for climate-friendly products. In this environment, Mesh businesses are poised to thrive, because they are based on using resources more efficiently. They use information-enabled sharing to extract additional value from physical resources—to turn waste into profit.

In fact, what two friends, the physicists Eric Wilhelm and Saul Griffith, called the hardware problem of climate change first inspired my thoughts about the Mesh. If we keep making carbon-intensive and disposable stuff on one end of the planet, moving it to the other end, and throwing it away, then the climate change problem becomes truly insoluble. One solution is to manufacture things closer to home. But the primary solution, the happier path, is simply to produce fewer, more thoughtfully designed products and to use them more effectively. Then, less will be made—and wasted.

The density of consumer information they receive enables Mesh businesses to manage resources (and waste) efficiently and well. Better yet, by sharing information about product and service usage by customers, families, and communities, a group of businesses can best identify ways to use products and by-products efficiently. Profitable services that reuse, recycle, and upcycle products will more easily emerge.

value
unused
=waste

In natural systems, waste is never wasted. In nature, "waste" from one system is food for another. The challenge in business is how to retrieve value from waste of all types, such as idle cars or equipment. It's finding value products that can be repaired rather than earmarked for the dump. The Mesh invites and enables the recovery of that "waste" as value.

Basin Electric Power Cooperative

During the Great Depression, rural electric development varied dramatically by country: France, Germany, and New Zealand delivered electricity to more than 60 percent of their countryside, but the rural United States was barely 10 percent developed. Investor-owned utility companies were convinced that building transmission lines to sparsely populated areas was too costly.

Then in 1935, President Franklin Delano Roosevelt established the Rural Electrification Administration (REA) and allotted $100 million to electrify the countryside. As expected, an overwhelming majority of investor-owned utility companies snubbed the idea. Instead, farmers formed electric cooperatives and worked directly with the REA to bring electricity to the countryside.

Originally, hydropower from dams provided the bulk of the electricity. But a disastrous flood on the Missouri River in 1943 convinced farmers they needed other sources of power. By 1961, they had formed a nonprofit, consumer-owned cooperative called Basin Electric Power to purchase, build, and manage power plants. Today, Basin Electric provides power to nearly 3 million customers in 135 rural member systems spread throughout Colorado, Iowa, Minnesota, Montana, Nebraska, New Mexico, North

Dakota, South Dakota, and Wyoming. It is one of one hundred rural electric cooperatives that serve 30 million Americans in forty-six states. Together they own and maintain nearly half of all distribution lines in the country, which cover 75 percent of the United States. Similar cooperative structures have also been thriving for decades throughout Canada and Western Europe. Many of them, such as Windunie, in the Netherlands, have expanded their services to include wind and solar power generation.

Government can help by creating incentives for improving energy efficiency and reducing waste. Denmark is encouraging the adoption of electric vehicles with heavy tax credits. In Canada, Ontario will give EVs special license plates to use HOV lanes and gain access to recharging stations. Since the 1970s, California has given residents credits for energy-saving moves such as installing solar panels. The state requires low-flow toilets and energy-efficient appliances in new homes—and recently passed a bill that allows people to share their cars while maintaining their personal insurance coverage. California's energy utilities have incentives to buy more alternative energy from local producers in order to meet their targets for nonpolluting energy sources. New state laws are also on the books to reduce driving and carbon emissions. These policies drive decisions by consumers and businesses, and in large part account for California's superlative record in energy efficiency relative to other states.

Governments, of course, have a long history of influencing energy policy. One of the most successful examples was the expansion, during the New Deal era, of electrical service to rural areas in the United States. Laws and subsidies stimulated the growth of rural energy cooperatives, which are still growing and expanding into new forms of energy.

Mesh businesses and legislators should consider designing incentives to encourage share platforms that reduce greenhouse gases. Instead of subsidizing gas, we could promote behaviors that support share-based businesses coming online and into the black. What about a tax credit for car owners who turn their vehicles over to an Own-to-Mesh car-sharing service, like Relay-Rides or WhipCar, full- or part-time? The service could then offer a substantial discount to participants, while substantially reducing greenhouse gas emissions. That's an incentive, too— for all of us.

a dense driver.

A million new people move to the world's cities every week. Two centuries ago, only 3 percent of the population lived in cities. The figure is roughly half of the population now, and expected to grow to over 60 percent in just twenty years. One reason, of course, is simple population growth. Also, the better-paying and more interesting jobs are in urban areas. Cities can operate more efficiently than small towns. They are transportation hubs, historically built close to natural harbors and rivers.

The massive migration to the cities is simultaneously creating greater density within urban areas. Many cities do not have the option of growing out. That land is long since taken, or is valuable as farmland and protected. Instead, cities will grow up, literally vertically. While density is still a dirty word with many people, there are many benefits to denser, more populated cities. In a word: amenities. More cafés, well-designed public spaces, taxis, transit stops, bike sharing, and restaurants. More cultural destinations. More efficient ways to move goods in and out.

Denser cities are the perfect soil for growing Mesh businesses. When there are more people nearby to easily access and share cars, clothes, or bikes, the service is more cost-effective and profitable. Partnerships are easier to find and execute. Share platforms such as restaurants, taxis, broadband wireless, apartment buildings, airports, and hotels are more profitable to expand in a denser municipal environment. No wonder that, even in the United States, walkable cities and neighborhoods designed along the lines of European "café society" have become more desirable. Real estate listings feature "walk scores." There's even a noticeable reverse migration from American suburbs back to the cities.

Urban areas with greater density are also fertile ground for clusters of related Mesh businesses to take root and grow.

Michael Porter at Harvard studies industry clusters, such as shoes in Milan, publishing in New York, film in Mumbai, and technology in Silicon Valley. In the *Harvard Business Review* he writes, "Clusters are important, because they allow companies to be more productive and innovative than they could be in isolation. [Clusters] reduce the barriers to entry for new business creation relative to other locations." The proximity of businesses in an urban cluster speeds up sharing of expertise and labor pools, makes opportunities easier to spot, and promotes cooperation around common market goals. The Mesh, which is built on sharing information, markets, and social networks, is particularly well poised to take advantage of these clusters.

Even some suburbs are becoming more Mesh-friendly. Early on, car-sharing companies chiefly targeted high-density locations with large numbers of college and university students. Those cities are the beachhead for expanding to other types of communities. Increasing numbers of suburbs have train or transit stations that can serve as hubs for bike and car sharing. Developers in northern California, for example, are constructing multifamily communities to support up to 3,000 people in both single-family homes and medium-density town houses. Many developments are organized around transit hubs. In this arrangement, residents can walk, ride their bikes, or drive shared cars to a train station, bus station, or ferry. There were eight to twelve cars in the garage with Mini Mucho, the share car I used in Vancouver. It's easy to imagine a multifamily community of two hundred or more homes supporting that level of usage.

weaving an ever stronger web.

The Mesh is made possible by well over twenty years of investment in the information infrastructure, and over fifty years of investment in roads and transit. We live inside a global network, with close to 5 billion mobile-phone subscriptions. Well over a billion people regularly use the Internet, which a Harvard business professor estimates has a $1.4 trillion economic impact annually in the United States alone. The network increasingly connects our homes, cars, and other devices, and they are increasingly connected to each other. (IBM recently introduced a kit that enables developers to use wireless sensors to connect *anything* to the so-called Internet of things.) And our demands are growing. Cisco estimates traffic over the Internet will exceed 667 exabytes by 2013. That's roughly 667 billion gigabytes and equates to a quintupling of traffic from 2009 to 2013. Cisco predicts that one trillion devices will be connected to the Internet by that time.

This invisible network enables a level of service and ad hoc coordination that is brand-new. That's how Spride Share helps riders share taxis, how OpenTable enables last-minute restaurant reservations, and how Groupon makes spontaneous, time-limited deals between groups of users and businesses. It's now hard to move around the planet without having mobile coverage. Sharing physical things is more realistic now that we've spent ten-plus years getting very comfortable with the always-on, always-with-me sensation of the Web and mobile devices.

The new connectedness has inspired and enabled companies to glean important data from customers to customize offerings—for iTunes to suggest songs, for example, and Linked-In to connect like-minded professionals seeking business opportunities and employment. Retailers such as Walmart, Costco, grocery stores, and drugstores are now trying to establish a direct relationship with the consumer. Stores give discounts to "members" with cards. When you use your card at the cash register, a store learns your family buying habits. Think of a Safeway card. When the scanner swipes the UPC code at the cash register, the software combines information from the transaction and the customer identity to make new offers. If you are buying diapers, the cash register will print coupons for wipes or spill-proof cups—products that you might purchase in the future. The retailer wants to up-sell you or extend what you would normally purchase.

Still, the collection and use of consumer data is in its infancy. In particular, manufacturers have had difficulty getting direct feedback from customers about product design. They often solicit information through warranty cards or online registration. Some pay attention to online ratings and comments on consumer sites. But these efforts have largely failed. At Kodak, we were lucky to get 1 percent of the warranty cards returned on our products.

The Mesh enables manufacturers to retrieve more useful information from customers. First, Mesh businesses *collect* more customer information. Second, as we've seen, they have a greater interest than traditional retailers in good design. They want long-lasting products that please customers over multiple uses. Traditional retailers generally prefer products with a short life span, so the customer will buy a new one. Third, Mesh businesses often purchase core products directly from the manufacturer, and lots of them. A bike-sharing company will typically buy many bikes. That creates the possibility for rich flows of information about customers between the bike manufacturer and the bike-sharing business. The result is well-built bikes that last, and with the features customers want. Aggregated information about the customer can also flow the other way, back to the customers themselves. Tripkick, for instance, accumulates consumer experiences about hotels to help users choose the perfect hotel room. Again, the greater number of transactions in the Mesh yields more precise and actionable information for all parties and parts of the value chain, from the manufacturer to the consumer.

The forces described here are unlikely to go away. The global population is growing, while resource scarcity and climate change drive up costs. The worldwide recession has bred distrust of old business models, but also openness to different approaches. The spread of integrated Web, mobile, and social networks is global, large, and accelerating. Mesh businesses, which use sophisticated information systems to profit from sharing resources, are ideally positioned to take advantage of these trends. Are you?

5

In Mesh We Trust

WHAT'S HERE: trust erosion, or sandbags and other customer-retention strategies; trials, the first date all over again; delight is contagious and so is its evil twin; caution when cussing at customers.

On almost certainly the last night that Sarah Kohl-Leaf will ever go to the St. Croix Falls Cinema in St. Croix Falls, Wisconsin, she tried to purchase movie tickets for herself, her husband, and two friends with a credit card. The ticket clerk told her the theater didn't accept credit cards, or debit cards, and she should use the theater's ATM. She tried, but the ATM was out of cash. Fortunately, one of her friends had a check, and was able to buy the tickets. Sarah, her husband, and their two friends took their seats, and that might have been the end of the story. But according to Sarah, five minutes after the film began, a member of the staff walked in and demanded to see everyone's ticket stub. The staff member suspected some people of sneaking in, and spent the next twenty minutes examining every ticket with a flashlight. While the movie played.

That night Sarah e-mailed the theater management. "I would rather drive to White Bear Lake, where they obviously know how to run a theater, than have this experience again," she wrote. Sarah's complaint landed on the desk of Steven Payne, a vice president at Evergreen Entertainment LLC, the owners of the St. Croix Falls Cinema. Here is his reply in full:

Sarah,

Drive to White Bear Lake and also go fuck your-self. If you dont [sic] have money for entertainment, get a better job, and don't pay for everything on your credit or check card. You can also shove your time and gas up your fucking ass. Also, find better things to do with your time. This email is an abso-lute joke. We don't care to have you as a customer. Let me know if you need directions to white bear lake [sic].

Steven

We know this was his reply because a friend of Sarah's cousin created a Facebook page entitled "BOYCOTT St. Croix Falls Cinema 8" and posted the e-mail exchange that Sunday. By Wednesday, the page had over 3,300 fans, according to a write-up in the *Minneapolis Star-Tribune*, and the number grew to over 5,500 within a month. The population of St. Croix Falls, Wisconsin, is 2,210.

Steven Payne, it barely needs saying, was forced to apologize. He suggested it had been a tough time of management tran-sition, and claimed to be addressing issues at the theater that had arisen without his knowledge. "At Evergreen Entertainment, customer service is an important part of our business," he wrote.

"Please accept my sincerest apologies for my actions, and I hope that this misstep does not affect your experience with Evergreen Entertainment in the future."

We can only speculate how much fun Steven had at his performance review at the end of the year. (Clue: the "We Support Steven J. Payne—VP of St. Croix Falls Cinema 8" Facebook page clocks in at 220 fans.) What we know is that in a pique, perhaps unaware of the power of social networks, he very nearly destroyed any faith on the part of his customers that their needs and interests would come first.

Earning and maintaining the customer's trust has always been important in business. But social and mobile networks have changed the equation, tipping the balance of power considerably toward the customer. In our highly connected world, practically speaking, a brand is defined more by how people experience it, and what they say about it, than what the company says about itself. Movie executives, whose films rise and fall on viral opinions spread through social networks, understand this new reality. When a movie comes out, they anxiously check sites like Skinnipopcorn, which collects up-to-the-second tweets about new releases. Ditto restaurant owners, whose Yelp ratings can float or sink them. Actions and stories about actions are potent, traveling far and fast. They are more relevant than sexy advertising slogans and PR claims harboring unfulfilled promises. In this environment, what people say about your company and your products continually redefines your brand. One commentator calls it the "age of radical transparency."

The challenge highlighted by the St. Croix Falls Cinema 8 story is that companies and their cherished brands must create and embrace teams, tools, and practices that enable a fresh, responsive, and authentic voice. The old strategy of carefully crafting the positioning and message, and then surgically pushing it out to the "market" to ingest as delivered, is, well, no longer being swallowed. The highly connected, engaged, and vocal world market will in fact shape how products, brands, and companies reshape and refine themselves. Twitter is an excellent example of a company whose product was immature and incomplete upon launch. But the founders had the wisdom to listen to passionate early users of their product to direct features, service terms, and focus. They haven't looked back since.

Through increased interactions, the Mesh offers more opportunities to win a customer's trust, and more occasions to put it at risk. Although trust is fundamental to any business, as it is to any human relationship, in the Mesh it's even more important. Trust is social, which makes all business social; Mesh businesses are hypersocial. When sharing is central to a company's core ethos, it must be constantly alert to the individual customer's evolving needs and proclivities.

Once customers' trust is earned, successful Mesh companies work to win and retain their loyalty anew with each interaction. Unlike a certain Wisconsin cinema, they prove themselves to be reliable, and serious about making good on a promise. They tap data from all sides to pay attention to the market, so that their team is conspicuously awake to new opportunities for keeping the brand and products up-to-date and delightful. These businesses nurture robust networks of trust. They cultivate loyal customers and "discoverers"—the early, vocal, and connected users—build the brand, weather tough times, and attract strong, brand-enhancing partners.

How do you foster trust with your customers, partners, and employees? Are you able to absorb dings when bad things happen? Does each interaction with your company enhance or diminish the trust people have given you? There are seven keys to building trust in the Mesh:

1. **Say what you do**—manage expectations and revisit them frequently.

2. Use **trials**.

3. **Do what you say.**

4. Perpetually **delight customers**.

5. **Embrace social networks** and go deep.

6. Value transparency, but **protect privacy**.

7. **Deal with negative publicity** and feedback promptly and skillfully.

say. do. win.

People relying on your service need to know one thing, first and foremost—that your business can truly deliver on its promise. The minimum standard of trust is based on reliability and fulfilling expectations, both outright commitments and implicit ones. When customers arrive at the car-share parking lot, the cars should be clean, well maintained, and ready to go. Customers want to know they won't be overcharged, and that the information about where they went or how long they were gone won't be shared with anyone (especially, it turns out, their spouses).

Customers want to know that they will have access to the service when it's needed. They don't want to be disappointed. Of course, expectations vary. If a customer uses a car-sharing service once a year to go on vacation, her expectation is quite different from the customer who needs a car available three times a week to do important errands. Professionals may require a higher level of attention than nonprofessional customers, even if they have to pay a premium charge. The likely outcome here will be for car-share companies to brand themselves entirely around one market segment or offer a menu of services to appropriately target each type of customer. If someone tries out a tool library in the neighborhood because he's curious about how to use a circular saw, it's not the end of the world if it's unavailable that day. But suppose the tool librarian said he had a router available, and the borrower needed it to complete a client's urgent project. If in fact the router is broken, or otherwise unavailable, the tool librarian is in what is technically known as deep doo-doo.

Keep your core promises to your customers, members, market, and partners—and start slow. A wonderful Indian restaurant around the corner from my office got unexpected preopening press coverage. They had a line out the door the first week they opened their doors. Great, right? As it turned out, no. True, the food was delicious, but the restaurant staff hadn't worked out the kinks in the kitchen or the front of the house. People waited an hour to get fed. Some of those customers will probably never come back. Worse, they may have shared their experience with a friend or made recommendations through an online community, such as Yelp. Unlike Vegas, what happens in the Mesh doesn't stay there.

For a Mesh business, there are a lot of details to get right to make an experience free of speed bumps. It's best to find first customers whose expectations are low and enthusiasm is high, not the kind of people who are easily irked or rarely amused. Because I'm an early adopter myself, I always say "early adoption" is French for "overpaying to have things that don't work." Still, in the Meshy world of rapid-fire social media, it's best to make sure things *do* work—and that free early-in-the-market tests are conducted with an appreciative crowd of friendly, candid supporters. Start small, win big.

trials, the first date all over again.

For most customers, trust-building starts with a small commitment. Mesh businesses are often nontraditional and unfamiliar. They fly in the face of ownership or classic financing. To get past potential customer reluctance, Mesh marketers can suggest promising trials, which are often the first step to engage a new member. Grocery stores offer samples, such as herbal goat cheese on crackers, for a reason—to win over skeptics. The same thing can work for bike sharing or peer-to-peer lending. Customers are likely to first try a Mesh business when it's least stressful to do so. They'll start by identifying things that they consider too expensive to own or keep. Someone may want to try a table saw or a hybrid car before going ahead with a purchase. Perhaps she has a closet half full of things she no longer wears. These are good places to begin testing the Mesh. Even so, many people will wait until version 2.0 or even 3.0 is refined before jumping in.

Mesh businesses can borrow clever new ideas for offering trials to customers. One trend is "tryvertising," where, instead of advertising, companies place products in people's daily lives. In some cases, people pay a small fee to get samples of new products, and then give feedback to the manufacturer. For only five euros, a Barcelona-based outfit, esloúltimo, allows customers to try out five products for two weeks, including a variety of food, household, and tech products. Tryvertising might be used to listen to a potential market and hone the offer, or simply to determine the market's preference for owning, as opposed to just using, new tools and services. This direct feedback loop entices

Mesh businesses to listen hard, refine the offer, and fulfill their promises.

Trials provide a perfect way for people to discover the joy of a Mesh lifestyle one product or service at a time. In the Mesh, offers are bite-size. Customers can reach a comfort level with a service before committing to let go of something they own. This "tapas" style allows the market to grow organically as potential customers respond to easy-to-accept offers. They learn to love the Mesh at their pace.

delight is contagious!

Let's imagine I'm starting a bike-sharing company with two kinds of bicycles. I plan on adding a third type, cargo trike, in six months. In that case, I'd better not sell people today on tomorrow's offerings. A better approach is to let early customers know that they're part of a business that's just starting and eager to engage with them. Solicit their input. What other types of products, tools, or services would they like to see? When the first few cargo trikes come in, I can offer them to early customers for a free trial and uninhibited feedback. I haven't overpromised. I've overdelivered. The likely result: wildly enthusiastic and hopefully vocal customers, and thoughtful, enthusiastic product reviews to share with my vendors. Earn the trust. Expand from there. Give more value than the customer expected for the time and money she spent. Tease out ideas for better service and mild complaints from happy customers rather than waiting for loud, unhappy comments with social momentum.

Beyond being reliable, the onus is on the Mesh business to consistently delight and even amaze customers. Blow them away with the service. Why? Well, Mesh businesses have the tools to give concierge service to everybody in their network. When customers engage with a Mesh company, they will likely tender information about their requirements, expectations, and desires—and potentially those of some friends and colleagues. Mesh businesses use that data to create an intimate transaction that makes them "feel the love." With the data a Mesh business can "micro-cast" offers to individual customers or small segments that cannot be well served by other companies. And as the commercial climate becomes increasingly competitive, customer expectations ramp up.

The richness of the information I can provide a Mesh business, as well as its ability to partner with other companies, gives that business a better understanding of who I am and what I need. It can then get it to me when I want it. With the infrastructure available to collect meaningful data about customers, the imperative is to make well-tailored, irresistible offers regularly. That's the core of what makes the Mesh payoff. Customers know the business is paying attention to them. Each transaction provides another chance for them to experience the brand and the service and renew that faith.

It's important in any business to make a customer feel that she matters. There are many good examples. A café knows exactly what type of overpriced caffeinated drink a particular engineering student likes before he steps up to place his order. A tailor or dry cleaner e-mails or texts a professor to let her know her clothes are ready. Amazon creates a "personal store" shaped by a book lover's past purchases and invites her to a special reading event. Netflix puts so much value in bubbling up "always better" suggestions for each customer that they run a $1 million contest to improve their recommendations formula.

When a company makes each and every interaction with a customer feel special, she will want to come back and share her delight with her friends. That's the Mesh standard—the aim is not to focus only on a single sale. It's to continually engage with the customer over her lifelong relationship with the brand and its services. When a customer has truly bought into a brand, the company will be the first to learn when something goes wrong. Customers' loyalty translates into their willingness to give the company a chance to make things right. They exercise their right to complain often, hoping that their trusted brand will step up and fulfill their expectation. At that point, there's another chance to wow them by resolving the issue promptly and well— to make them feel smart and back in the trust boat again.

A discussion in business that has annoyed me outright over the last ten years is about who owns the customer. Often this emerges when two companies are negotiating for a partnership or copromotion. One company will typically claim to "own the customer." Even the phrase strikes me as absurd. In my view, the true "owner" is no one and everyone, but ultimately . . . the customer! A business has to earn the right to the relationship with each new transaction. Customers' histories with the company provide valuable information about what is likely to make them happy. That gives the company a leg up over the competition. But it doesn't ensure you of anything once the person leaves your store, online or on the street.

nurture big mouths.

Recent studies have confirmed what many of us have known now for some time—advertising is significantly less effective in cultivating new customers than word of mouth. WOM, as it's known among marketers, is the powerhouse behind winning over new hearts and wallets. The biggest and best introduction to any business is always through family and friends. Other customers can also be very influential. If somebody who genuinely likes a company or service shares that feeling with people in his life, that's a huge business driver. Social services like Twitter, Facebook, MySpace, Hyves, Bebo, and orkut and platforms like Elgg, Drupal, and Xing have turbocharged a historically effective way to enhance a brand, expand a market, and drive new sales.

As noted earlier, certain people act as discoverers or influencers among their social circles. Typically, someone deep in music or food or gadgets is out in front, researching, exploring, and recommending them to friends. Discoverers who are early affiliates of a business may come to feel that their connection to the brand is part of who they are. They have a sort of spiritual ownership. They become very natural spokespersons for the business, and serve as a trust filter in an authentic way.

At Ofoto we often noted that the people who took the photos, uploaded them, and shared them with their friends were not the same people who printed the most books or cards. The photographers provided beautiful scenes from parties and trips and inspired their friends to indulge, further share, and spend time creating photo books. Our "authors," as we called them, were extremely loyal to our business and brand. They continually demanded and then were pleased by upgraded tools available to enrich and share their photos. These authors, especially in the beginning of our business, were our lifeblood. They pushed us into their homes and into the hearts and minds of their social network.

Mesh businesses should engender an appreciation and love of the brand, or service, with these key influencers. Encouraging these discoverers to act as trust agents on behalf of the business is a smart strategy and one that often flows naturally from early adopters' engagement of the service and support of the brand. Any business can create rewards for a person who's acting in that role.

Social networks and influencers in friends and family networks can help Mesh businesses get out of the gate. They can kick-start customer trials that generate genuinely good feedback. "Brand echoes" can be prolific and phenomenal. A product or business can become popular, and fast. Someone can blog about a brand or service in a positive way. It can get picked up on Twitter, and then other people re-tweet it. In a matter of months, Curtis Kimball's popular Crème Brûlée Cart in San Francisco attracted more than 11,000 followers on Twitter. They love his crème brûlée so much that they tweet each other to share exactly where the cart will be, and what flavors are on the menu.

Like Curtis, Mesh businesses can use the age-old tactic of "offering product samples" while encouraging prospective customers to tell their friends, in this case about the decadent dessert they luckily encountered. Social media coupled with product samples provide the type of broadcast benefits that digital products enjoyed when music or video could be sampled and then shared online. This is really the first time that physical products—crème brûlée!—can appreciate the same type of leverage.

out in the open.

Traditionally, many businesses haven't wanted you to know anything about how the sausage was made. Transparency with customers was avoided, sometimes aggressively. But that attitude is changing rapidly. Certain users demand to know more. They want to understand what they're signing up for. They want to know more about the record of the inkjet printer they're considering—is it cheap to buy but expensive to maintain?—and where their clothes or cleaning products are made. People want to know if companies are abusing people, animals, or the planet. They want to know where their food comes from, how it was prepared, and what's in it, for reasons of health, ethics, the environment, religion, and even taste.

Ideally, a Mesh business should strive for transparency in what it's doing, with whom, and why. The current reality is that very few relationships, personal or business, are fully transparent, and for many reasons. Transparency is a little tricky. A business might not want to share certain information because it's personal either to the business or to other customers.

My trust or distrust of a company partly revolves around how my personal information is handled. While most people want to know how their information is used, people's perception of the relative importance of privacy varies. While I'm not super keen on giving out a lot of information about myself in exchange for goodies, there are a lot of people who will do so quite willingly. The requirements for privacy, interestingly, tend to be different for people in defined demographics. In particular, young people often have different attitudes toward privacy than their parents or grandparents.

Companies should be guided by "permission marketing," a concept described by Seth Godin several years ago. The basic idea is this: if a customer exchanges personal information for something offered by the company, she should get back more than what was given. When I say that I trust a business with my personal information, I expect it to convert that information into real value for me. I want it to understand what I need, and to trust that it can and will deliver. Companies that take advantage of that principle are going to win in a big way.

A study at Carnegie Mellon University determined that half the users in a survey were willing to pay more for goods on Web sites that had better privacy practices—an average of about 60 cents more on a $10 purchase. The percentage shot up for what the researchers called "privacy-sensitive products," such as sex toys. The moral: Mesh businesses need to take privacy concerns seriously, because their customers and partners do.

Any Mesh business that trades customers' information without asking permission to do so undermines their trust. It's also not up to the business to share who else in a customer's Facebook network, network of friends, or zip code is also a member of the service, unless each person grants permission to do so.

Some users are very concerned about protecting their private information. Google's version of a social networking site, Buzz, was slapped with a class action lawsuit because they made users' personal information public. Ditto Facebook. When the social networking site changed its default privacy settings, there was a howl of protest. Some users tried to remove themselves from Facebook entirely. The company ultimately blocked a Dutch outfit that charged people a premium to remove them from the social networking site. And in an almost comic case of brand extension, Wisk, the laundry detergent, has created Wisk-It, a Facebook app that enables you to pull your tagged and untagged photos from the site.

going negative.

Shortly before Thanksgiving in 2009, I got a worried call from my dad, who lives outside Philly. "I saw something just now on TV," he said. "There's a big braking problem with Toyotas—you better get it checked right away." I owned a Prius. I loved my Prius. "Right, Dad, thanks. I'll check it out," is what I said. What I was thinking was: right, Dad, and don't believe everything you see on TV. Still, I gave the Web a cursory glance for something about Toyota braking problems, and found zip. Then my dad started sending me links. Apparently, the floor mat was causing the accelerator to stick, speeding Toyotas out of control.

Before the braking story broke, Toyota was at the top of its game. The company had been voted the world's most valued brand of vehicle, ahead of BMW, Porsche, and Mercedes. The year before, it had become the largest car manufacturer in the world, surpassing GM, which had held the title since the Great Depression. But as the story unfolded, the death count mounted. At least fifty-six people have died. Over 10 million cars have been recalled.

Toyota misled Congress and the public. It had known about the problem at least two years before it became public. Overnight, Toyota's reputation for reliability plunged. Kelley Blue Book decreased the resale value of recalled vehicles, reflecting a drop in consumer demand for Toyotas. After the problems were revealed, sales fell 16 percent in the first month alone. It will take an extraordinary effort for Toyota to regain the public's trust, a loss that will be reflected in its customer satisfaction ratings, technical safety ratings, and sales for years to come. Personally, I look at my Prius now with more trepidation than affection. My trust in Toyota has been called into question.

Especially since the recession began in 2007, mistrust has emerged as a latent vulnerability for many old brands. We know that bad things do happen in business. When they do, companies, unlike Toyota, must deal with them promptly and deftly. Today, pretty much anybody can say anything about a business. Some people, whether on Twitter, Facebook, a blog, or some other media format, can be extremely influential. If they go negative on the business, especially if they have good reason to go negative, then how the business rebuilds trust is crucial. Here are some general rules:

1. **Pay attention.** Condé Nast used to have an ombudsman for a travel magazine it published. People knew that if they had a terrible experience with a hotel, airline,

agency, or anyone in the hospitality business, they could seek assistance from the ombudsman. The ombudsman would publicly embarrass the company in the magazine and shame it into making good. Since everyone with an Internet connection can publicly broadcast reviews, the ombudsman is *anyone* now. Successful businesses have people from marketing, customer support, and product development tapped into their customers' comments, suggestions, and complaints. These companies know that this pulse, this interaction, is the life force of their brands.

2. **Act now.** By the time you figure out who said something negative and whether it was relevant to you, it's probably already spread on the Internet. There are probably ten other people who commented negatively; they've re-tweeted that sentiment, and in a flash it's gone. If you get to it late, and people perceive that your company is not paying attention, one person's comment could generate hundreds or thousands of negative messages.

3. **Be boldly honest.** Companies still hire PR firms to spin the latest product recall or CEO gaff. But increasingly, if a company tries to conceal a mistake, or BS about why it happened, people's caca-meter goes to 11. In 1982, an unknown person or persons laced Tylenol capsules with potassium cyanide and placed them in supermarkets and drugstores in the Chicago area. Several people died, including a twelve-year-old girl. Rather than play down the incidents, Johnson & Johnson widely distributed warnings, recalled all Tylenol products (an estimated

31 million bottles worth $100 million), and warned people in nationally televised advertisements not to use its products. Product share dropped to 8 percent, but it rebounded in less than a year. Johnson & Johnson was widely praised for how it handled the incident, and the event affected the public relations industry's subsequent attitude toward leveling with the public. When bad things happen, companies should simply come clean immediately. They need to explain how the problem will be corrected. Honesty allows people to give companies another chance. Being straight with the public builds trust.

4. **Don't panic, and keep perspective.** Acting quickly doesn't mean panicking. Individuals cannot be running around freaking out every time somebody says something negative about them. Companies are the same. Building trust involves knowing not only what criticisms are being leveled by customers but also who the speakers are, and how, or if, to respond. Almost every service, whether it's Target, Virgin, Yelp, Amazon, or Joie de Vivre Hotels, has reviews. Of a hundred reviews of a hotel or restaurant, most may be four stars, but some of the reviews will inevitably be negative. A few people say, "That food was inedible," or "The waiter was surly." It's true that a series of bad reviews on Yelp or Zagat can be deadly for a local restaurant. On the other hand, when consumers go to look at reviews, they are accustomed to seeing a range of ratings. And many people have learned to evaluate the evaluators. If the reviewer is a twenty-one-year-old who apparently likes to stay up late and

make a lot of noise, he may be disgruntled because a hotel's management told him to keep it down. Or the reviewers may be a seventy-year-old couple who wants quiet, and no late-night activity near their room.

5. **Pay special attention to people in the network (aka your customers).** When people are members of Zipcar or a food co-op, they are inside a network. They've already bought into the vision of the service and are part of a community. If an issue arises, they will usually work to resolve it. They have something at stake and are biased toward mutual success. The stakes are also higher for the business. If a customer is mistreated and complains about it on Facebook, the company has not only lost a subscriber but potentially soured relationships and its brand with a broader base. Unfortunately, sometimes people in competitive businesses do pose as subscribers to complain about a rival company. The good news is that when a company acts fairly, it'll usually get another chance.

bad behavior and personal brands.

What happens when Mesh customers act badly? This is a concern voiced by those who argue for the advantages of ownership. What if some guy who uses a shared car before me has a kid who throws animal crackers all over the seat? He was supposed to leave the car like he found it, full of gas, not animal crackers. If I had gotten to Mini Mucho and it had animal crackers all over the back seat, I would have considered it a bad first experience. I would have called Zipcar, and considered it a serious inconvenience.

With Zipcar and other Mesh services, how members treat the cars, tools, bikes, or homes in circulation will inevitably affect other users. I've been guilty of leaving empty plastic water bottles and newspapers in rental cars as I took off sprinting to catch my plane. There will be these kinds of mistakes, but there will also be people who choose not to play by the rules. Services will likely build in a reputation system to identify these "high-risk" users and charge them more, or restrict their choices. These businesses will find a balance point where the rights, rules, and pricing of their offering will match their market and encourage best practices. But part of the Meshy experience is feeling part of something. People tend to be a little bit more conscious. Misbehavior is less likely to happen when people feel part of a community network. In 2009, Elinor Ostrom and Oliver Williamson were awarded the Nobel Prize in economics for their groundbreaking studies of how effectively groups of people govern "the commons" they share. Ostrom carefully researched long-standing community-managed resources, from Swiss grazing pastures, to Japanese forests, to irrigation systems in Spain and the Philippines.

A friend of mine got an instructive demonstration of community behavior when he was hired by the Brazilian electrical utility to help deal with a chronic problem. Residents in the urban favelas routinely divert electricity to their homes, costing the utility millions of dollars. The company had launched various crackdowns to no avail. My friend found that the residents didn't regard taking the electricity as stealing: it's only stealing if you take from a friend. To them, the utility was a distant power that they didn't know or trust. My friend suggested that the company become more involved in the communities to build trust. He cited the Brazilian subway system, which has little theft or gate jumping. The transit authority does catch violators, but they don't send them to the police. Instead, they work with neighborhood organizations called *juntas de vecinos*, which enforce the rules. If there's a fine, the *junta de vecinos* pays it. The difference between the utility and the transit authority is that the subway officials have invested trust in communities, and get it back in return. For the Brazilian transit authority, and for Mesh companies, maintaining trust and a good reputation with customers reduces bad behavior and creates a buffer if it happens.

Beyond the social pressures that come into play in the Mesh, financial pressures can also be brought to bear. If someone borrows a book from the library and returns it in crummy condition, the librarian might roll her eyes and make a note-to-self. But in a car- or bike- or tool-sharing system, where the same physical good is reused by a relatively small community of people, the business can ascribe a value or cost to the condition in which things are returned. Over time, Mesh businesses can reward good behavior and/or levy taxes. They can lower rates when something comes back in pristine condition, and raise rates for members who are harder on the goods than other people and therefore increase maintenance costs. Mesh businesses may create segments of customers according to the way that they behave with the goods. The price point will be relative to that. The cost-effectiveness will gradually come to a rightful balance, on a member-by-member basis, because Mesh businesses will have access to the information on a user's "performance."

Of course, Mesh businesses should do everything to encourage the sense of community that rewards direct feedback and discourages bad behavior from customers. If a business is successful in building that feeling among their members, it will be richly rewarded in myriad ways. Trust me on that.

6

The Mesh as Ecosystem

WHAT'S HERE: meet you in the cloud;
find a niche and go stand there; your
customers are your customers' customers;
the rediscovery of how; don't nap, adapt.

In 2006, a documentary film called *Who Killed the Electric Car?* managed to draw popular attention. The film featured Hollywood celebrities such as Tom Hanks, Alexandra Paul, and Ed Begley Jr. celebrating and then mourning their EV1 electric cars. GM had used the celebrities to road-test the cars, and then abruptly taken them away. The film indicts the auto and oil industries, as well as officials in California and the Bush administration, for crushing a promising low-emission technology. Toward the end of the documentary, the filmmakers track down the parking lot where the reclaimed EV1s are marooned. There, the camera captures some dramatic, *60 Minutes*–style shots of Alexandra Paul and other protesters being arrested as they try to block the huge trucks carting the cars off to be demolished. Certainly, it was not a fine moment for the cause of innovation in the United States, or for the country's auto industry, which already had an environmental black eye over their gas-guzzling SUVs.

But it's also true that the number of elements and parties that have to come together to create a mature, economically viable technology like electric vehicles is daunting. University and private researchers, government regulators, and industrial competitors have to share information and common purpose. The political and commercial will has to be in place to spur the creation of an entirely new infrastructure to support the vehicles. Despite these obstacles, there are signs that the parts of the puzzle may finally be coming together, led in part by a Palo Alto–based company called Better Place. The CEO, Shai Agassi, says he named the company in response to the simple question posed at a World Economic Forum meeting in Davos, Switzerland: "How can we make the world a better place?"

Better Place has managed to attract several partners for different pieces of the electric vehicle puzzle, or as I like to think of it, the EV "ecosystem." Better Place's primary role is to create and run a network of battery-switching stations. The EV pulls into the station, which looks similar to a car wash, and a robotic arm replaces the nearly depleted battery for a recharged one. For short-term city driving, there will be compact charging stations located at customers' residences, and in parking lots, retail locations, and other convenient spots. Better Place has partnered with Renault to build the cars, and with various governments, including those of Denmark, Australia, and California, to support the infrastructure development. The company planned its first launch in Israel—where a thousand charging stations have been installed, with more to come—followed by Denmark.

The EV infrastructure requires standards, much like the Internet. Agassi's model was the mobile phone, where drivers would pay for miles the way phone users pay for minutes. Like phones, the creation of design standards for the battery-powered cars is a crucial piece, and difficult in the auto industry, where traditionally the only fuel standard required has been the diameter of the hole for the gas pump. Success depends on operating systems that can speak to each other and coordinate a complex series of actions seamlessly. No wonder Better Place has focused on building the EV's operating system. The company was conceived inside the technology sector, where Agassi was formerly a top exec with the enterprise software giant SAP. In fact, like many Mesh businesses, Better Place is best viewed as an information company. The data required for the system to function smoothly, and the data it collects to improve the service, is the primary share platform. This sets up nicely for the Better Place network to offer value-added services, traffic reports, directions, efficiency analysis, and feedback to manufacturers to improve EV performance. The operating system is the backbone for the shared physical dimensions of the company, including the batteries, the switching stations, and the energy sources.

Better Place is not only a Mesh business, but the hub of what I refer to as a "Mesh ecosystem." A core strength of the Mesh is the ability to fully integrate clusters of partners and systems for sharing information.

spice up your Mesh. get partners.

As mentioned in chapter 1, the multiple transactions involved in Mesh businesses also expand partnership opportunities. For an entrepreneur, part of the joy and excitement of the Mesh is that it opens up new ways to build partnerships, make offers, and bring products to specific markets with tools that haven't been supplied together before. Young brands will find sweet spots very quickly.

They will attend to niche markets or local communities and make intersections among entertainment, food, or other services.

Classes of services, like transportation and travel, are opportune for organizing Mesh ecosystems. (A personal favorite: to prevent drunk driving, Heineken has partnered with taxi companies in major cities to create Taxi Magic, a free online booking service.) Homeexhange.com might pair with RelayRides, Spride Share, or WhipCar to offer their customers a deal on a local car service. Roomorama, as I noted earlier, makes lodging arrangements with film festivals and conferences. Perhaps they could add a bike-sharing partner, or use consumer data to figure out what nearby restaurants or events might appeal to the filmgoers.

Of course, bike sharing alone is a fine thing. But the richer opportunity is to collect similar brands or interesting coconspirators to create an ecosystem of services—everything from other kinds of sports equipment, to a tool share with bike wrenches, to a hostel association—for selected customers. The businesses within the network achieve greater value by thoughtfully integrating with other services. Over time, the partners will have more and more data to create ever more personalized offers. Partners are attracted to Mesh ecosystems to provide products and services to like-minded audiences, where the voice, tone, package, and price point all appeal to that market.

Integrating information from your own and other systems allows companies to offer better service to a particular flavor of customer. Since the Mesh is interactive with all parties—the company, the community that it's servicing, and the partners—the information is fresh (and in some cases, its value is perishable). These businesses have the fuel to create new incentives or expectations, continually shaping their offers, and therefore their brands. That's when access truly trumps ownership.

Mesh businesses can also expand their horizons by playing

with unexpected partners. Most people think of AARP as simply an organization that supports older people. But AARP is also effectively a marketing organization targeted to an interesting and important community. For a Mesh business such as home sharing or mentoring and education, partnering with AARP could be a ticket to reach millions. Every offer isn't going to reach millions of people right away, or perhaps ever. Still, Mesh businesses can be imaginative in creating offers that make sense for shoppers who now gravitate to big-box retailers.

Mesh businesses are in the very early stages of developing ecosystems to serve markets. One of the entrepreneurial thrill rides of the next decade will be watching and helping these businesses develop mature ecosystems for partnering, sharing information and materials, and serving customers.

find a niche and go stand there before someone else does.

The ecosystem metaphor contains several elements useful to Mesh businesses. Nature operates in integrated systems. The true value lies in how all the elements of an ecosystem work together to sustain life over time—measured in millennia, not fiscal quarters. Here are some of the ways a Mesh ecosystem mimics a natural one:

1. Nature is not only integrated, it abhors a vacuum. Niches are quickly identified and filled, a crucial competitive strategy for Mesh businesses.

2. Nature is resilient and adaptive. Seasonal changes and catastrophic events may disrupt the pattern, but new

life emerges. Existing businesses also become more
resilient and sustainable in a Mesh ecosystem.

3. In nature, "waste" is food. Waste from one system
becomes food for another—it's never wasted. Vegeta-
tion and animals decompose to make fresh soil. Forests
absorb carbon dioxide and exhale oxygen; we do the
reverse. These processes are efficient. A Mesh ecosystem likewise evolves to simultaneously and efficiently
utilize and replenish available resources.

spot-weld that niche.

Since their information infrastructure is better able to identify
customer needs and desires, Mesh businesses easily find and fill
viable niches. The Virgin Group, for example, is good at creating
its own competition. It starts many, many businesses with the
expectation that they don't all need to work—Virgin Media,
Virgin Mobile, Virgin Music. Recently, it created a cab-sharing
service in New York and London called taxi[2], which is free to
passengers of any airline. Virgin execs like to just throw the spa-
ghetti on the wall to see if it sticks. They're looking for niches
that are fertile beds for high-value customers and future juicy
markets.

Prosper, the peer-to-peer lending firm, discovered a niche
opened up by the banking crisis. With people's confidence wan-
ing in the big banks, some turned to Prosper as an alternative.
Also, as the market restrained smaller banks from making local
loans, Prosper was able to fill part of the gap. Some of the banks
themselves turned to the company for help.

Niches often occur when customers are restless about current choices, as they were with the banks. Similarly, Etsy is a craft exchange that grew after finding a specialized community of customers on eBay a few years ago. A big challenge for a company like eBay is to retain early and important customers while trying to scale to get more. Companies deal with this issue in different ways. EBay acquired PayPal, which enhanced its platform, tightly integrated its core transaction services, and provided a whole new world of data to its merchants. The company also expanded regionally and into vertical niches, such as the wildly successful eBay Motors. But as it grew, eBay could offer only limited customization to smaller audiences.

Etsy's founders took advantage of this business phenomenon. They noticed that there were a lot of crafters on eBay who make jewelry, clothing, housewares, gifts, hats, and specialty items. They were buying, selling, and talking to each other, and were keen to create a crafter-centric experience. Etsy identified the crafters as a growing niche and launched a platform crafted specifically for them. Etsy charges crafters less money than eBay does but still makes an impressive profit. It's a good example of a company that basically says, "I can cater to your special needs better than those bigger folks can."

Etsy found a niche and created a Mesh-style share platform for a community of creators. A disproportionately high number of members of the Etsy community are also buyers within the community. In this way, they recirculate money back to the community, empowering other crafters. Members share money, knowledge, and the crafts themselves. Crafters get together to make co-offers such as, "I'll make a hat if you make a sweater." Or, "I'll throw the jewelry in if you make that outfit." Etsy is currently working toward more robust social networking. Say a guy in North Carolina is looking for a gift for his wife, and she really likes llama wool.

Prosper

By 2006, Chris Larsen saw the makings of a perfect storm. Borrowers in the United States had gained access to their credit scores for the first time a year earlier. A few years earlier, a nationwide electronic funds transfer system called the Automated Clearing House (ACH) came online. Social networks were taking off. The stage was set, Chris thought, for profitable peer-to-peer (p2p) lending.

Having just sold a venture, E-Loan, Chris cofounded Prosper, a p2p lending marketplace, with more than $40 million in venture capital funding. Prosper offers a convenient and transparent way to get a personal loan or invest in loans on terms considerably more favorable than those banks are offering. Prosper's registered members request loans or bid on them through an online auction platform. Perhaps someone is starting a landscaping business, or a family is paying for their daughter's college tuition. Borrowers describe how they will use the money and denote the highest interest they are willing to pay. After considering the borrowers' personal stories and proposed return, lenders select loans from the listings and bid on them in increments of $25 to $25,000. Once an auction ends, Prosper notifies the winning bidders and consolidates the bids with the lowest rates into one simple loan for the borrower.

Prosper is now the largest such institution in the United States, but it experienced a major speed bump along the way. The Securities and Exchange Commission (SEC) made an early investigation into Prosper's core offering to determine if the company should be required to comply with banking regulations. Prosper argued that it was a marketplace, not a bank, and should not be required to keep a certain percentage of money on hand relative to the number of loans it issues. After a year of inquiry, the SEC's investigators agreed.

In the four years after the company's launch in 2006, Prosper's 930,000 members had funded $190 million in loans. It is one of the many thriving p2p financial ventures, including the first of such marketplaces, Zopa, which is based in the U.K. and has expanded to Italy and Japan. All facilitate individual loans and offer significantly higher rates of return than traditional banks. In a recent article, *American Banker*, a notable trade journal, acknowledged this advantage in recommending p2p lending as a compelling asset class for diversification of investment portfolios. Other p2p financial companies, such as Lending Club, SmartyPig, BigCarrot, GreenNote, Kisskissbankbank, auxmoney, and smava, have entered the field, often focused on a particular geography or type of customer. The p2p funding tree is growing fast.

The company will direct him to crafters with llama wool products, including those who raise llamas and spin and hand dye their own wool.

Make magazine, a spin-off of O'Reilly Media, defines a related niche. Although they tend to operate independently, Makers comprise a vital, exciting community, of which crafters are a subset. From a traditional market perspective, Makers have been considered fringe, but they are good fodder for Mesh businesses. They host an annual Maker Faire. It is a phenomenal weekend event that brings Makers from all over the world together with other Makers, Maker wannabes, and Maker appreciators. Many are good early adopters—they can usually put up with setbacks and laugh them off. The community includes people interested in robotics, architecture, clothing, food, parachutes, bicycles, and many other things. They think about the built environment, energy, and transportation. The world of people who are passionate about how to design, make, repair, and embellish things is zooming along. Hackerspaces, for example, are sites that support those who want to start or join a local community where people share a physical space, equipment, and ideas for working on projects.

There are even emergent communities among the Makers, such as the growing DIY (do-it-yourself) group. A company called Instructables has built a simple method to demonstrate DIY hardware projects, with the idea that if people could get better at making stuff, then they would buy, and import, less stuff. Chris Anderson, editor of *Wired* magazine, argues that traditional product manufacturers will feel pressure from do-it-yourselfers who have readier and less expensive access to sophisticated tools for designing and making things. DIY may also benefit certain Mesh businesses by removing financial and logistical obstacles to creating new products and services, or repairing and improving old ones. Even though it's a tiny percentage of the market, the DIY community has grown substantially since 2005.

tell me where it hurts.

Mesh businesses can also find niches within a market by looking for points of pain for the customer. The Mesh is a game changer. During the transition, entrepreneurs have opportunities to create smoother surfaces along the way—to make sure that substitution is not sacrificial. Here's an example. Imagine a father who wants a car so he can drop off the kids at school before heading to work. He figures he'll have to walk to the car-share location from his house with his kids, their bag lunches, the car seats, movie from Netflix, and whatever else. That takes the convenience out of the whole process, even if the car is two blocks away. What if there was a way to store all those things at the pickup spot? Maybe Netflix could deliver directly to the father's little share box or mobile tablet. Perhaps a nearby vendor offers healthy lunch bags for the kids. These niche services would help remove the dad's problems with using the car-sharing service.

The number of Web sites and apps that make sharing easier is growing. Expensure is a free and secure tool that helps people who live or travel together to securely track, manage, and resolve shared joint expenses quickly. The tool resolves a common problem for people who are sharing rooms, cars, tools, or virtually anything else. As people start making a shift toward the Mesh, smart businesses like Expensure are able to see the impediments that discourage individuals or markets from using Mesh services. For entrepreneurs, these points of pain become hopeful and glaring niches of opportunity.

don't nap. adapt.

Mesh businesses are resilient. They're structured to adapt quickly and well to new conditions or consumer desires. When an individual owns a bike or a home, changing the model or the location can be difficult. Mesh businesses can offer a different bike model or expand the available locations for vacation homes with relative ease. As technology, government policies, fuel types, airfare prices, or other conditions change, Mesh businesses can adjust their offerings. Since they are thoroughly integrated with their partners and customers, they can iterate and adapt quickly and well.

Frequent, transparent contact with customers and partners equips Mesh businesses to spot problems, trends, and opportunities early. They can then respond rapidly to strengthen customer trust, or update their offerings. When hybrid vehicles came onto the market, there was a significant amount of customer skepticism and resistance to jumping in with both feet. People were reluctant to be the first to buy. Mesh businesses allow new products like hybrids to be introduced more like tapas—as a sample first. Then if the product is well received (or preferably irresistible), customers can use it regularly, and tell others about how fun and easy it actually is to use.

Like with any business, the early enthusiasts are big allies. The added bonus in a Mesh business is that the threshold to engagement—what a customer needs to get over the hump of using a new product—is significantly less than a full-on purchase requires. Even for traditional businesses looking to sell products, a Mesh-style offering can lower resistance to new purchases. A share service may be the business's version of tryvertising—a way for customers to have a taste of the EV, say, without a big financial commitment upfront. The lower threshold to engagement produces less stress for the new customer, and gives the business an opportunity to get feedback from several customers in a short time.

Consider thredUP's adaptation to those short, expensive people that its initial customers were living with (also known as children). The company's initial base of satisfied adults with new swapped, button-down shirts let them in on a little secret: kids require full-on wardrobe changes on a regular and mostly predictable schedule. In other words, the little buggers are expensive. Voilà! It defined a high-value, big-market need that isn't going away any time soon. ThredUP listened and learned. It leveraged the platform it had already built, and then relaunched with a whole new focus. In that way, it kept most of its original customers while gaining shorter ones, too.

waste equals food.

Most business people understand that, no matter what country you live in, there will be financial consequences for creating or harboring waste, whether in the form of energy, garbage, or squandered natural resources. A number of countries, now including the United States, are increasingly requiring manufacturers to upcycle, reuse materials, or pay for disposal of their products. Today, all businesses strive to optimize the value chains where products and services are created and brought to market. In the future, I expect equal attention to be given to the "reverse value chain"—reclaiming the value of the recovered product or its materials. Manufacturers, retailers, and regulators are already starting to focus on devising systems to create value from products after their initial use has expired. A new infrastructure will develop for products to be upgraded, supported, maintained, and repaired. This is a big shift, and it's coming soon, bringing big new opportunities (and consequences) with it.

Waste represents the underutilization of existing resources. In business, there's a technical term for the efficient employment of physical assets—yield management. Each flight of an airplane, for instance, requires a certain financial outlay, regardless of how many passengers it carries. The pilot, stewards, and maintenance personnel must be paid whether there are 7 passengers or 270. The fuel cost and wear and tear on the airplane are the same. Once the plane takes off with seven passengers, it's gone, and so too are its costs and profits. Airlines have used various methods to increase the number of passengers on each flight (unfortunately including overbooking). Mesh businesses can maintain superior yield management. The density of consumer information they receive enables them to manage resources (and waste) efficiently, regularly, and well.

In fact, recovering and sharing raw materials and natural resources is a critical part of the Mesh. Sharing steel parts, or the steel itself, is at least as important in the Mesh as sharing cars. Earth, after all, is the ultimate share platform. The waste-is-food moniker applies with added force to the ecosystems of Mesh businesses. Key partners that aren't necessarily involved in making a visible offer to the customer will instead use the "waste." Business-to-business enterprises are rapidly emerging that reuse and recycle parts and materials. Many manufacturers, with government encouragement, are starting to upcycle their product at the end of its life, to be deconstructed for parts and materials. RecycleBank, for example, partners with cities by offering credits with participating businesses for recycling goods. The organization reclaims old devices and materials, and makes money from the cities by lowering the bills for putting trash in landfills.

As discussed earlier, in a Mesh ecosystem products are *designed* to be maintained, high performing, and serviceable. Businesses will find niches for maintaining and servicing products. Bike-sharing companies may offer their own repair and recycling services. Usable parts would be refurbished and reused efficiently to maintain the bike fleet. Others would be broken down to recover constituent materials, such as steel and rubber. Alternatively, businesses that offer those services may grow up around the bike-sharing companies. In either event, the company's purchases would be guided as much by what happens on the back end of the value chain as on the front end.

The business-to-business cluster that develops inside a Mesh network will have other long-term advantages. Businesses rather than individual consumers will make many of the purchasing decisions. A tool-sharing service will buy a lot of tools. As tool sharing scales up, these companies will be better able to define what different groups of customers want, which in turn will influence their own buying decisions, and ultimately what manufacturers offer. While based on consumer feedback, including data on how the tools are in fact used, tool-sharing companies will have more clout and communication with manufacturers than the individual consumer. And these companies, like all Mesh businesses, will want products that are durable, can be more easily serviced, and have parts that can be recycled.

Beyond businesses and governments, many individuals also understand that global ecosystems are being compromised. They know that the fascination with buying new stuff and then throwing it away cannot be sustained. In response to this concern, consumer-facing companies have invented clever ways to reduce and reuse waste. One I like is Rickshaw Bags, which has made packs and purses using recycled plastic soda bottles, most notably from Coca-Cola. They've also designed a clever and colorful pouch called the Round Trip Shipper. After one of their products arrives in the mail in round-trip shipper packaging, you apply the enclosed prepaid postage label and drop the pouch back in the mailbox. LooptWorks is a retailer that converts waste into material that is usable in clothing and other gear. JGoods offers customers a "sneaker restoration kit" to get more life from their sneakers, which I count as a kind of personal upcycling. There are also apps, including Freecycle, ecofindeRRR, Earth911, and, in the U.K., reuze and Recycle Now, that help you find where to recycle almost anything. Some retailers offer consumers a small amount of money or credit for recycling older models. The offer is: Bring in your old device. We will recycle it and give you 20 percent off your next purchase. The retailer builds loyalty and takes a baby step toward repositioning itself as a service-oriented business.

Like businesses, individuals can also achieve better personal yield management through the Mesh. WhipCar and Couch-Surfing allow an individual to get more use for only marginally greater cost from his car and, well, couch. This personal yield management relies on information and information tools available to the individual through association with a Mesh business—yet another advantage of access over ownership.

custom design for all.

Further, in the future, customers can help determine how their Mesh ecosystem is put together. When I've talked to people who are involved in food co-ops, one of the things that people love is the ability to heavily influence the selection of products and vendors. The phone services company Credo asks its customers to choose to which worthy causes it will donate a percentage of its profits. Even as Mesh businesses form partnerships in a local area or among similar customers, your ecosystem will likely come together in a very different way than mine. The way the businesses talk to you will be based specifically on what you need and what you've asked for.

Best of all, as Mesh ecosystems improve and mature, they will not only mimic nature's use of waste as food. They will literally help preserve and restore nature's ecosystems, making all of us a little richer.

7

Open to the Mesh

WHAT'S HERE: and then there was a
network, and it was open; what's that
you're hiding?; open up and make good
things happen faster; expecting
transparency; early in, we all benefit—
later on, I may want my toys back.

In the late 1990s, two young architects, horrified by the plight
of war refugees in Kosovo, reacted in a conventionally humanitarian way. They wanted to help. But the way the young couple
chose to respond was far from conventional. They created a network, and an innovative way to share ideas, that engaged their
fellow professionals. That network, Architecture for Humanity,
has unleashed the inventiveness of thousands since its founding in 1999. Similar types of networks, where information and
resources are more freely shared, can take Mesh businesses to
warp speed.

The couple, Cameron Sinclair and Kate Stohr, began simply. They created an open design competition to build homes
for the refugees. To their surprise, hundreds of ideas poured

in, including one for building new structures from rubble, and another for low-cost, inflatable hemp huts. Next up was an initiative to build mobile health clinics in Africa to combat HIV/AIDS. Again, architects all over the world responded. One designed a rotating clinic that begins with planting kenaf seed. The edible plant grows fourteen feet in a month. In the fourth week, the doctors arrive. With the villagers, volunteers mow out the clinic space, a sort of crop-circle office, and add a lightweight roof. When the docs have done their work, the village eats the clinic.

Great ideas flowed in, and also created a problem. The architects wanted to make it easy to replicate the best and most appropriate designs throughout the developing world. But they were concerned that some company might take the free blueprints and make a profit building from them. With the Internet, this problem has become a common concern for creators. How do you share intellectual property without your work getting ripped off or used for unintended purposes?

Architecture for Humanity turned to Creative Commons, an organization developed by Larry Lessig, a law professor at Stanford. Through a fairly simple licensing mechanism, Creative Commons has enabled intellectual property to be shared widely under terms decided on by the creator—over 130 million works have been licensed in 50 countries since 2002. Options include completely free use, free use only under restricted circumstances (typically only used for nonprofit purposes), and an option similar to ordinary copyright. For the architects, the Stanford group designed an elegant solution, the Creative Commons Developing Nations License. Use the design for its intended purpose, no problem. Use it outside the developing world to make a profit, pay royalties. A combination sports facility and HIV/AIDS clinic in South Africa was the project built under the new license.

and then there was a network, and it was open.

Then Architecture for Humanity went an important step further. To facilitate the widespread sharing of good ideas, they devised what is perhaps their greatest innovation, the Open Architecture Network. (The TED Prize, won by Cameron Sinclair in 2006, largely supported the development of the network.) Architects and other designers can now freely collaborate over the Internet by sharing, and archiving, their best ideas. Not only architects, but also communities and NGOs (nongovernmental organizations) can use the resource to design appropriate local projects. Design, Architecture for Humanity argues, is the ultimate renewable resource. Today, they have 40,000 members in eighty chapters in twenty-five countries that participate. Their cheeky slogan is "Design like you give a damn."

Why create share platforms where ideas and information can be freely shared? Once the core offering is refined, traditional business logic dictates that a more proprietary approach will distinguish you from competitors, and create protection against them. Individual creators and companies have long built businesses and fortunes by registering patents and enforcing secrecy. General Electric controlled the patents on lightbulbs, invested heavily in plants to manufacture the bulbs efficiently, and made profits by cranking out the bulbs for decades to follow. Sony, Kodak, HP, and many others played this game and won. In the case of Kodak, George Eastman even decided to own the cows to make the gelatin needed for the film emulsion. That way, no one's pictures from a birth, graduation, or wedding would be ruined because of contaminated gelatin from an outside vendor. Mr. Eastman's view at the time was that Kodak should be directly responsible for all aspects of quality, since the quality of the photographs would make the brand. In addition and over time, the company's profits increased by taking out its vendors, or buying them.

Proprietary control carries significant advantages, especially once a business or category reaches a certain size. Owning intellectual property, including manufacturing processes, enables companies to establish a substantial defensive barrier against competitors. In fact, corporations often signal dominance in a category by controlling the ideas, and the relevant supply and distribution chain. Nor is the proprietary model limited to older companies. Successful brands such as Apple, Facebook, and Google employ similar strategies. While some of their platforms provide developers and customers with important collaborative tools, they are careful to guard what they regard as their core intellectual property, including customer data. They buy potential competitors. or use their size to eliminate them.

With proprietary control, a company can more directly manage its supply chain, exercise quality and cost control, and reduce risks. It has historically gained greater influence over industry regulation. And it removes some of the risk from scaling up. Before you invest a lot of money in creating factories and distribution channels, you want insurance against someone taking your idea or potential profits. When Lexmark, Epson, HP, or Sony make printers that accept only their own cartridges, they fend off competitors in supplying ink and make a higher margin on their proprietary cartridges.

But across-the-chain proprietary control carries significant risks of its own, and can be a hair-raising ride on the way down. Over time, it erodes the trust of customers, whose choices have been constrained. The business is no longer about growing a category or serving a market. The goal is simply to optimize gross profit and extend the life of the rapidly maturing category.

life cycle of mesh businesses

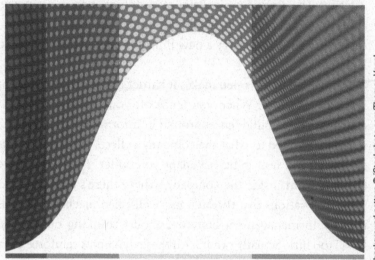

infancy   adolescence   adulthood   full maturity

Mesh Companies in Various Stages of Growth.

This makes the brand vulnerable. Proprietary ink cartridges may generate customer resentment that a competitor can exploit. If the competitor makes a better offer, the customers are likely to jump at it. As we will see in the next chapter, that's exactly what happened in the movie rental market.

The erosion of a brand also limits its extensibility. When customers trust a brand, they're more willing to try a new product offering. The reverse is also true. If customers become annoyed at paying exorbitant prices for Brand X's printing cartridges, they're far less likely to try a new line of monitors that the brand launches.

Worse, being less open makes it harder to keep the product or service up-to-date. When you fence off your intellectual property, others also build fences around it. Information on a specific market is limited to what the company collects. That means less feedback, and less ability to adapt your offer. New ideas have to come from inside the company, where there's a tendency to resist innovations that threaten its "well-oiled machine." For all the talk in management literature about "thinking outside the box," too little actually occurs. All these dynamics reinforce each other, speeding a downward cycle.

early in, we all benefit. later on, i may want my toys back.

On the other hand, there are plenty of examples of how openly sharing ideas and information has significantly accelerated an industry's development. Although the Internet and social networking tools have hastened adoption of open development models, the idea isn't new. In nineteenth-century England, owners of blast furnaces shared technical and economic information about the furnaces in trade journals and trade association meetings. Rapid rates of innovation and productivity improvement resulted. A similar result occurred in New England paper mills in the early 1800s, as well as in other industries.

A more recent example, of course, is open software development. By sharing ideas and code, engineers around the world have rapidly improved the architecture, overall performance, and security of software. They quickly develop new versions and debug them. Social networks further speed up development times. In some cases, very large corporations, such as the German software giant SAP, are using social networks to actively involve their customers to spot problems, suggest improvements, and serve as a help desk for other users. This service is also available through third parties. Get Satisfaction is a peer-to-peer customer service that provides support for companies such as Zappos, Nike, and Microsoft—but can be great for emerging Mesh businesses as well. The platform, recently made easier to use through a Facebook app, helps companies create robust interactions with their real and potential customers.

The advantages of sharing information, and even platforms, are particularly evident in the "define" and "refine" stages of a company's development. Increased knowledge of who customers are and what they really want eliminates a lot of waste in manufacturing a product or setting up a service. Marketing is better targeted, less expensive, and more effective. In the Mesh, sharing information with partners in the early life cycle of a business builds momentum, support, and trust for your idea, product, and brand. Shared information promotes rapid iterative definition and refinement of your initial offering. By vetting the idea, you not only create a better offer, but also avoid costly mistakes. And you can go to market faster, for less money. The trust gives your brand energy, strength, and flexibility that can help you well into the future. Both openness and trust enhance your ability to add and adapt future offerings that keep your products and services fresh, along with your brand.

The public ethos is also changing. Companies perceived as closed and proprietary are more likely to be disfavored by customers, potential partners, and even regulators. People suspect these companies of doing something that the companies don't want them to know about. Transparency telegraphs, "We've got nothing to hide, so you can trust us." Particularly in the newer, faster-moving, more information-saturated business environment, becoming more proprietary may in fact strongly signal that a company is headed toward the end of its life cycle.

Many Mesh businesses are at the beginning of their life cycles, when sharing of ideas and information have clear advantages. I've seen up close how open architecture can drive hyperinnovation, while creating a greater sense of community. Mozilla, where I have been an active friend and adviser for years, is perhaps the best example of that ethos, system, and commitment. Mozilla developed the browser Firefox to create a better Web experience. Many of us were concerned about one or a few companies controlling the *channel* that has become the Internet. Firefox's intellectual property is held under a special type of open-source license. The code, developed by community and incorporated into Firefox, continues to be held by those members, who in return grant access to Mozilla to embed and use it. This "communal IP," as I call it, is a wonderful example of the share economy ethos that was, and hopefully will remain, at the core of the Internet. Mozilla, Creative Commons, Wikipedia, and Architecture for Humanity remain strong embodiments of that ethos. The result is continuously organic improvement of the Web experience for all. These open communities and platforms are a terrific demonstration of the culture of gifting and generosity that fueled the "Web economy" in the mid-1990s. I believe it remains central to nurturing the next generation of healthy social innovations.

No one can say for sure whether Mesh businesses will continue to stress openness as they mature. As the businesses grow, some are likely to seek an edge by becoming more proprietary. What I do know is that enormous competitive advantages flow from sharing information and ideas, particularly in a Mesh ecosystem among partners and communities. The Internet itself is the best example. Sharing, transparency, and trust play well together. Their ethos, intent, and approach are well aligned. And when these three are aligned, they have the power to change industries and more.

8

Mesh Inc.

WHAT'S HERE: Netflix slays a movie dragon;
hit them where they thrive; five flavors of the
big mesh; how to build a bigger box; take a
geek to lunch.

When people ask me whether major corporations can join
the Mesh, my short answer is: many already have. In fact, Mesh
corporations of considerable size are thriving. Several others,
including some of the world's fastest-growing companies, have
adopted full or partial Mesh strategies to win market share and
increase profits. Still others have created platforms and services
that make it easier for Mesh businesses to start and thrive.

Even companies that are purely based on selling can adopt
Mesh strategies as a way to introduce their customers to new
products. A "Mesh division" of a jewelry company, for example, might arrange for a group of preferred customers to share a
newly designed line of necklaces and earrings in order to assess
their popularity. Those customers who were particularly enamored of the new design could then buy the products. Over the

longer run, the company may learn that the Mesh division cultivates richer customer relationships and is more profitable than sales. Without having established the division, that profit and knowledge would have been lost, perhaps to a Mesh competitor.

Of course, many companies won't embrace the Mesh. Their business models might be currently working just fine to generate shareholder profits. The necessary cultural and technological shifts may be seen as too wrenching or costly. But corporate executives ignore the Mesh at their peril. The competitive advantages the Mesh offers in today's information-soaked environment will pose a persistent and growing threat to traditional business models. I had a front-row seat as the Internet uprooted earlier models. I sat in business meetings where major executives resisted or denied what was happening. With the Mesh, it's déjà vu all over again.

Netflix slays a movie dragon.

To illustrate, let's return to Blockbuster Wayne Huizenga, as I mentioned, grew highly profitable enterprises by recognizing the advantages of share platforms. Whether he was dealing in Dumpsters or videos, his core strategy was to invest in products that customers could use over and over again. He acted on the advantages companies gain through multiple transactions with customers. Through its chain of stores, Blockbuster collected information on what videos were being rented, and in what areas, which allowed the company to efficiently manage its stock. Through Blockbuster club memberships, the company kept in touch with customers and rewarded them with discounts. Blockbuster outgrew its competitors (many of which copied their basic strategy), and looked set to dominate the movie rental market for years to come. Then it all came tumbling down.

Netflix used what I'd call a textbook Mesh strategy—if a Mesh textbook existed—to beat Blockbuster. First, Netflix paid close attention to Blockbuster's vulnerabilities with its best customers. Netfix knew that Blockbuster's Achilles' heel was late fees. Blockbuster's revenue model depended on the fees, but customers hated them. Late fees were irritating to pay, like parking tickets, and created anxiety around running the videos back before the noon deadline. Worse, its best customers were the most likely to be punished by the fees. Netflix realized that if it could create a profitable business model that didn't require late fees, it'd win.

The then-in-progress shift to the DVD format presented an opportunity. Netflix realized DVDs could be safely and inexpensively delivered by the post office. Its customers wouldn't have to rush down to the rental store, hoping that a new release would still be available. They wouldn't have to wait in line behind a guy arguing with his girlfriend, only to reach an underpaid clerk who'd clearly rather be somewhere else. And they wouldn't have to pay a late fee, because there weren't any late fees. Instead, Netflix introduced a subscription model that allowed customers to watch and return movies at their own pace.

What clinched Netflix's advantage, though, was that it functioned as an information business. By creating a Web-based share platform where people could buy a subscription and queue up their movie choices, Netflix executives knew they could really get to know the customers. Early on, Netflix began using a customer's prior selections and ratings to suggest other videos that might be of interest. As the service developed, the company added layers of information to inform a user's choices, such as reviews from people in the network whose profile of selections and ratings were similar. Recently, it sponsored a contest awarding a million dollars to anyone who could significantly improve the movie recommendation service. Thousands of teams from more than a hundred nations competed. Netflix's "recommendation engine" relies on algorithms culled from masses of data collected on the Web, including that provided directly by customers. The lesson learned from the contest, according to the *New York Times*, was the power of collaboration, as winning teams began sharing ideas and information: "The formula for success was to bring together people with complementary skills and combine different methods of problem solving." The result was an improved engine for sussing out consumer preferences, and a marked increase in their satisfaction and retention. Very Meshy.

Netflix also included ratings and reviews from newspaper critics and customers. Over time, more social networking functions were built in to allow friends to suggest movies to each other. The Web site encouraged customer feedback on improving the service, and continually introduced new tools to make it easier to find, rate, and order movies and TV shows. Rather than conducting expensive national advertising campaigns, Netflix created partnerships with nearly every brand of DVD player. Each new player included a card offering three free DVD rentals from Netflix. The card also made a promise: "No Late Fees."

Instead, Blockbuster paid a late fee. They were late in acknowledging customer resentments, and late in understanding the spreading power of social networks to shape brand perception. They created a share platform, but neglected other elements that make Mesh businesses so competitive. Netflix's more robust and networked share platform gave it the power to collect and crunch consumer, usage, and product data to shape customized offers. Its service is delivered locally, but spread through social networks, partnerships, and word of mouth. With its more nuanced knowledge of customer preferences and its culture of

	low ← data-enabled goodness → high
share a lot ↑ frequency of sharing ↓ **share a little**	subways / hotel rooms / taxis / museums / parks — iTunes / Netflix / Zipcar / Amazon Web Services — toaster / toothbrush / teacup / socks — notebook computer / mobile phone / GPS device

Data-Rich, Highly Shareable Goods and Services Mesh Best.

innovation and trial, Netflix can rapidly adapt offers to particular communities and markets. These are classic Mesh advantages. And in a business blink of the eye, Netflix replaced Blockbuster as the dominant player in the category. In the future, the byword will be "convergence"—of TV, the Internet, and mobile devices. Netflix remains well positioned to compete in that arena as a sophisticated information company with a trusted brand.

five flavors of the big Mesh.

Not all large companies can adopt a Mesh strategy as thoroughly and successfully as Netflix. Many can, will, and have adopted aspects of the Mesh where they're able to perceive the competitive advantages. Here are five ways:

1. Provide services or platforms that enable and encourage Mesh businesses. We've already discussed several, such as Amazon Web Services, PayPal, and FedEx. Like many other companies, the streaming music service Pandora extends its service through an iPhone app. The iPad, Kindle, and Kno are strong new platforms for distributing e-books, blogs, video, and magazines. These services are likely to be reshaped in even more favorable ways by the Mesh as it grows. A very important category of Mesh-enablers is the social networks, such as Twitter, Buzz, MySpace, LinkedIn, and Facebook.

2. Leverage physical assets, both products and materials, as share platforms. Ask: How can I get a better yield from the physical assets we own, including the materials that go into our products? How can I

turn waste into value? Mesh share strategies enable companies to extract more use, and more profit, from their products more of the time.

3. Truly engage partners by mutually sharing resources and information—including customer feedback and other data on their preferences—that enable better designed, more timely, and more relevant products and services. As Better Place demonstrates, the most important innovations often can't be done alone.

4. Integrate the supply chain, in forward and reverse. Tight integration of a distributed (not vertically integrated) supply chain increases efficiencies of cost and time. It often improves the quality of raw materials, and the product or service to be integrated. Walmart has driven its suppliers to thoroughly integrate using shared software and data platforms. These systems—and years of data—allow the company and its suppliers to review and analyze many aspects of their businesses over time. This sets Walmart and like companies up for a number of Meshy improvements: more energy- and resource-efficient practices; movement toward a profitable model for repairing and reusing products, not just selling them; and the related establishment of a "reverse supply chain" for recycling and upcycling parts and materials. In fact, Patagonia is already helping the big-box retailer green its supply chain—for free.

5. Extend the Mesh ecosystem. Hotels can easily integrate car and bike sharing into their suite of services.

Virgin's taxi[2] program is a partnership with a taxi-sharing service. Kimpton Hotels and Six Flags are just two of the many companies that have partnered with Zipcar to reach common markets. A good example of a distribution partnership is World of Good (textiles, bags, and jewelry made in developing countries), which uses Whole Foods stores to extend its reach.

networks of Meshworks.

In a very short time, Facebook has become the dominant social networking platform, with nearly 500 million users worldwide. It arguably has more relevant and textured information on its users than anyone else. What's more, Facebook has created a share platform that is brilliant for hosting new Mesh businesses. Like Amazon, it has grown its own company by providing an expanding list of tools that enable other businesses and organizations to build and serve their audiences. Facebook, one of the best-known and fastest-growing brands in the world, is largely built on a Mesh foundation.

Google, the other Internet giant, also uses Mesh strategies with several of its products. Google Maps has become a crucial, widely used share platform for many businesses, consumers, and nonprofit organizations. The maps provide location data—such as directions to the nearest bike-sharing outlet—that are crucial to many Mesh businesses. Google Earth is another share platform, continually improved by users through network services. And information available on Google Earth is often the basis for coordinated real-time action in the physical world. Jane Goodall, for example, uses the platform with the company's Android phone to monitor forests and wildlife. Information-enabled, user-influenced share platforms and community trust-building are core features of the Mesh.

test-drive Mesh elements.

Even without going Full Mesh, there are a number of ways for corporations to leverage physical assets—including the materials used in their products—as share platforms. Goodyear, for example, could migrate from selling tires to creating a tire service. Embedded chips could monitor the wear and tear on tires, and feed that information to both driver and company. Rotated tires could be swapped out to other vehicles to maximize their life cycle, and worn-out tires recycled into new ones or other products. (As we've noted, several governments are instituting requirements on many manufacturers to take back and upcycle the parts and materials in their products.) In this model, Goodyear would establish a long-term relationship with customers, enabled by mobile and data networks. They'd also help move their image toward more environmental responsibility, another trust builder.

complete the feedback loop.

Another Mesh strategy involves using data networks to seek more frequent and layered interactions with current and potential customers—and then using the information to improve products and services. Companies can and do use third parties to accomplish this. Flextronics is a publicly traded company that specializes in distributed manufacturing on behalf of technology companies. It coordinates the manufacture of products by

Dell, Motorola, HP, and many other brands. In recent years, Flextronics has started to collect information from end users to suggest product design changes on behalf of its clients. Manufacturers' products are mostly physical ones. The richer the interaction with customers, which Mesh strategies facilitate, the better and more competitive these products will be. As the product design improves, customers will use their social networks to recommend the product or brand.

Flextronics has ventured into upcycling as well. In the European Union and many other countries globally, it offers value-added services that enable customers to properly dispose of their electronic equipment. Customer-involved product recycling of this type can include refurbishing and reusing parts, as well as recycling constituent materials. Using information networks to facilitate materials sharing—such as making attractive offers over the Web for customers to participate in upcycling products—is basic Mesh.

how to build a bigger box.

Walmart is the largest retailer in the world. The company—and many other retailers hammering away on the same chorus—sells many cheap, throwaway goods. Consumer products with short life spans populate our landfills. And moving those goods across the globe and country burns energy. True, Walmart is taking steps, and setting a good example, to reduce its carbon footprint. But a bigger, Meshier opportunity lies before them and other big-box retailers.

Walmart, Dixons, Costco, Target, Media Markt, Next, Best Buy, and other big-box retailers are poised to take advantage of a richer part of the value chain. They could move from being huge retailers to becoming huge product service and repair providers. Walmart and other big-boxers could become the center of gravity for the conservation of goods, employ people with actual know-how, and develop deeper, longer term, more profitable relationships with their customers. Perhaps the big-box retailers can make friends with the Makers, Hackerspaces, and Instructables communities to establish a global repair business.

Most of Walmart's business, of course, is selling stuff. It sells a customer the cheapest TV or toaster today, expecting her to come back in a few years to again buy the new model of cheap TV or toaster. But every part of the value chain—manufacturing the toaster in China, shipping it, warehousing it, stocking it, and disposing of it—involves considerable waste. That waste is lost value that will become more and more visible on the bottom line as its costs rise. Setting aside the inevitable costs of climate change, or any future carbon taxes, a considerable part of that waste is in fossil fuels that are becoming scarcer, more costly to extract, and higher in price. That's a significant risk to Walmart's current business model, one that company itself is beginning to recognize.

What if, instead, Walmart guaranteed a customer the best-priced TV and toaster way into the future? If the TV breaks in three years or five years, Walmart repairs it, or offers upgrades that are less expensive than buying a new one. At the end of its life, the company reclaims the old TV, upcycles the parts and materials, and offers the customer a discount on a new one.

Members of a "Walmart Share Club" could be given a special password to a daily online auction on used equipment certified to be in good working condition. The auction would include many items that other customers traded up—customers grateful for a way to deal with unused consumer electronic devices that they don't know what the hell to do with. REI, for example, has had success with offering a discount on new skis when people return their older ones. REI then refurbishes the old skis and offers them as rentals.

A shift toward access and service would deepen the big-box retailer's relationship to customers, and win their loyalty. People will look to them not only for the best price but also for reliable service. After all, people buy electronics expecting them to function. When they don't, it is, at the very least, a big bummer. A service focus would bring more rewarding, frequent, and lasting contact with grateful customers. It's fundamentally a different business model, with additional rich profit.

take a geek to lunch.

Best Buy has already taken a step toward the service model. Its Geek Squads travel to people's homes to set up or repair equipment purchased in the store. This service business provides a real margin to Best Buy, and creates customer loyalty. The visits are occasions to sell upgrades and ancillary products or services. When a member of the Geek Squad services a home or business, there's an opening to say, "You're running your Macintosh or your Intel processor with an outdated operating system. I can do a firmware upgrade." That is, you can spend $300 to make this older computer work better for another year, rather than spending $1,500 on a new one.

Over time, a service like the Geek Squad encourages retailers to buy products that are durable and can be easily repaired. That sets the stage for a "reverse" supply chain, where the same careful attention to efficiency in supplying goods is applied to their recovery and reuse on the other end. To be reclaimable, the materials would necessarily be nontoxic.

Suppliers, partners, regulators, and even competitors will increasingly be required to design these reverse supply chains. Those industries and countries that are successful will be on the leading, not the tail, end of the twenty-first-century economy. And they can help each other thrive. Patagonia has long been a leader in environmentally sustainable business practices. In the process, it gained considerable knowledge about "greening" its supply chain. Now Patagonia is again showing leadership by sharing that knowledge with Walmart by helping it develop a product-specific sustainability index. And as we've seen, there's considerable evidence that customers appreciate businesses that take environmental concerns seriously, and make purchasing decisions accordingly. The economics of efficiency—of conserving rather than squandering resources—are also compelling. Both factors will drive up a Mesh or partial-Mesh company's earnings per share.

grab your partner.

Of course, the service model works best in a Mesh-style ecosystem, where information and resources are shared among partners. Mesh leaders, innovators, and provocateurs like Patagonia that share information with ecosystem partners will lead the path to the new economy and stimulate a "Mesh-ripe" culture. Since older businesses tend to feel they "own" their customers, and don't want to share data, they will find it increasingly difficult to compete with new Mesh businesses that have less resistance to sharing information. Although they may have less data to share in the beginning, Mesh businesses use that data to create more customized offers. Some large businesses, as we've seen, will find Mesh partners. Mesh businesses can also seek traditional business partners that help them reach bigger markets or realize economies of scale.

Even on their own, businesses both enormous and boutique can gain with Mesh strategies: create share platforms for goods and materials, devise and use rich data flows to refine your offers, and cultivate social networks to grow respect and reach for your brand. These are tricks even an old dog can learn.

9

Seed Your Own Mesh

WHAT'S HERE: make the everyday
better; arrive early, stay for the main meal;
define, refine, and scale; leverage the "now,"
grasshopper; finally, give serendipity a big
squeeze.

> **Don't worry about people stealing your idea. If it's
> original, you will have to ram it down their throats.**
> —**Howard Aiken, U.S. computer scientist (1900–1973)**

When you start any business, choose something that's gotten under your skin. It should be something you're passionate
about and willing to obsess about at weird hours. It could be a
market that you really love and think needs more attention, or a
kind of product or activity that you're enamored with. It could
be something you know could be done better with products or
services that are disruptive, edgy, game-changing, or honed to
precision. Right now, there are seemingly endless opportunities,
leveraging the Web, to create richer, deeper experiences. Web
services and platforms, from Amazon and Google to Twitter and

Facebook, are powerful business enablers that are cheap or free to use. Today, start-ups require less of some things (teams, tools, cash, owned infrastructure) to start up, just as the resource-wasting costs of traditional models are rising. With the recession, old brands have lost some ground, and people are more open to new ones. It's a brilliant time to launch a company, begin courting a customer base, and propel a new brand.

make the everyday better.

The Mesh offers some special opportunities, as we've seen. Here's how I'd start: Look around at your everyday life. First of all, most of us live in communities, transport ourselves on foot, bike, car, or public transportation, have families, go to work, socialize, make dinner, hang out, play, and exercise. All of these are rich fodder for Meshing, either from the customer side of the equation or from a material goods perspective.

For example, you might hear someone complaining about her commute, and how difficult it is to coordinate with family members when going to and from different meetings or venues. Perhaps you have the same issue. That's an opportunity to think about how a Mesh model might work better. As you start seeing the world through a Mesh lens, you'll notice opportunities to improve the customer experience, and to improve your own opportunities for business reach or leverage. You'll perk up when you hear something from a friend like, "We have this opportunity. We own a building I inherited from my family, and would like to explore some new ways of using it." Real estate, in fact, is one of the very fertile arenas for Mesh models to go to work. Consider thinkspace, Cubes&Crayons, and In Good Company. Each of them brings a different twist and fresh approach to office space and services.

Mesh business opportunities exist in pretty much every aspect of life, whether it's home services or child-care services, health care, fitness, food, or real estate. With your Mesh lens on, you'll also start to wonder: What is it I own, or my friends own that we value, where the relationship between the value and the relative cost is off-kilter? And can we form a community around offering that asset? Here are four things to ask yourself:

1. How could a physical asset be managed using technology that allows an entrepreneur to offer and track the asset?

2. What would you need or want to know about the customer that you wouldn't need if you were selling something outright? What type of partners might offer data to enhance your *peripheral* vision?

3. What kind of promise of service or maintenance is required for the business to thrive, and what kind of risk are you asking the customer to incur? How could you uniquely reduce or eliminate that risk?

4. What are you seriously passionate about?

With these questions in mind, here is some general advice for creating a Mesh business.

identify shareable physical assets.

Identify activities that require high-cost materials—a car or a bike, or a really cool handbag (like the ones offered by Rent the Runway or Bag Borrow or Steal). For consumers, personal transportation, food and shelter, office space, and real estate are good places to look. I would include services like gardening and building renovation, where expensive tools are involved.

RelayRides, Spride Share, DriveMyCarRentals, and WhipCar are good examples. These companies have their own spin on car sharing. They take advantage of the fact that lots of people already own their cars by letting owners offer their vehicles through the network. Cars sit in a driveway or parking lot most of the time. RelayRides customers sign up for the service in a way that's similar to a vacation exchange or a rental. The car owner logs into the network, says when and where the car will be available—preferably where the renter can find it!—and makes the keys available. RelayRides adds the car-sharing infrastructure, including insurance from State Farm. (This insurance company has shown a willingness to innovate in Meshy ways. A State Farm iPhone app enables customers to look up policy information, record accident details, and even submit claims with iPhone photos of the damage. A GPS feature, available to anyone, helps users find services, such as a nearby gas station, hotel, or towing service.)

Here's another example. In my hometown of Napa, there's suddenly a big garden space in the middle of town that no one knows what to do with. Some years ago, the Mondavis and others founded a museum and center to celebrate food, wine, and the arts, called Copia. It was quite a spectacular complex in the old town of Napa, along the river. But from a local's perspective, the wine exhibits, restaurant, and small shops weren't compelling enough to warrant repeat visits. Copia wasn't really hitting the mark, and it went bankrupt in 2008.

Copia remains a beautiful and well-equipped building set along the Napa River in the midst of a wine-and-food haven. Its enormous organic gardens are not only productive but also

spectacular. A number of different characters have been negotiating to take it out of bankruptcy. In the process of all that
negotiation, the community, which is full of people who are
enthusiastic about food and wine, and the restaurateurs, who
are finely focused on the quality of the raw ingredients that they
use, proposed a Meshy concept. The gardens are to be maintained by and for the use of the Napa community. People can
learn how to garden there, and also grow food for the local
restaurants—organic, local, and specialty stuff. The chefs will
direct what gets grown in different seasons, and then present
the harvest in their world-class restaurants. Copia's future is still
in flux, but there are no shortages of ideas on how to integrate
this treasure into the hearts and stomachs of the community and
its many visitors.

Whether we live in suburbs, cities, towns, or rural places,
there are land and real estate opportunities like this one. Who
is going to contribute to, and who's going to get value from,
these various assets or material goods? Landshare in the U.K.
and Local Dirt in the United States are good examples of services that match aspiring growers with landowners. Land uses
change over time. And the Mesh supports changing, adaptive
models.

People are now hypersensitive to the drag of the true cost
of things relative to their real and perceived value. That creates
opportunities to take advantage of the current real estate slump.
Citizen Space in San Francisco is a good example. A group of
people got together to create a shared workspace. There's also one
at the David Brower Center in Berkeley that is part of a worldwide network called the Hub. Both are interesting models, say, if
I am writing a book and want to be out of my house, but don't
necessarily want to take a huge office and sit by myself. I can sit

with people who do similar work or minimally have a similar work style. Or I can have a separate space where I can work but still pop out and take a walk or get a coffee with an office mate. Depending on the offering, you could have access to the space by month or by year. As a commercial building owner, these models expand the possible options for marketing, pricing, and attracting a range of tenants. More options can help an owner get through market fluctuations with less panting and chanting.

I would add another possibility for dreaming up a Mesh business—things that are consequential businesses or services related to going from ownership to access, such as financing, insurance, and maintenance. These are adjacent businesses that provide necessary services or reduce the "friction" of certain offers. Finance, insurance, and maintenance are fundamental for launching car sharing into the mainstream.

arrive early. stay for the main meal.

In most businesses where technology is involved, including Mesh businesses, there's something called the first mover advantage. You get the first mover advantage by, well, being first—by identifying a category or a class of service or product, and going to market with it before anyone else. If you do, you're often more likely to set the standard for the product or service expectations, build your brand, and be a partner magnet. Patagonia got ahead by branding a recycled textile for their clothes. Zynga is winning in social gaming, and Nike won by marketing an athlete's running shoes to weekend warriors and anyone who imagined themselves walking quickly one day. Of course, it's not always the case that whoever's first wins. Friendster blew its lead in social networking by crashing when traffic overloaded its site, and Microsoft used its advantage in owning the most widely used operating system and pushed Netscape aside with Internet Explorer.

Mesh businesses that are first have an additional factor to consider. Since they often deal in physical assets, they're not as easily changed as Web sites. At Ofoto, we could easily test and launch several different product designs in the same month. Kodak and other camera manufacturers needed a three-year cycle to define and build the product. Hardware, such as electronic devices, bicycles, cars, trucks, complicated appliances and equipment, and serious tools, take longer to design and manufacture to scale. The capital involved, the energy involved in making them, and the transportation to move them around is more costly in every way. That's why it's even more important at the beginning to engage with customers frequently—to learn what they really want and need before hitting the "scale up" button. Mesh businesses are especially well positioned to learn early and often by continual market engagement (tryvertising) and redesign of the offering. They aim for making regular, cheap, and high-value mistakes relative to those in traditional models.

define. refine. scale.

My little riff, which anybody who's worked with me for the last fifteen years is sick of hearing me say, is "Define, refine, and scale." With any business, Mesh or otherwise, you define the market and the core offering. You start to play with people who are your early adopters, and then refine your business offering, approach, and model. You are informed by how people really see the offering, what they compare it to, how they value it (or don't), and what they'd like to see modified. These interactions are golden, and they are not to be taken completely literally. Investors, partners, and customers may not grok fully what you see. It's our job as entrepreneurs to create passionate engagement with people around our vision—team, customers, partners, investors, and even the friends who have to listen to our stories over and over.

That moves you into the refine stage. After you've iterated and refined, you understand the market better. You understand the sorts of characters that you need on your team and the kind of capital that you might need in a competitive space. Then you scale. You push it out in a substantial way because you feel strongly that you've got a tight package and good cred with your initial customer base.

If you have an existing business, discover aspects of your business that may be shareable for different parts of your customer base. In general, people in existing customer bases are more likely to embrace change and try new things. By encouraging feedback from customers and developers, Mozilla refined its offerings and created a steady stream of applications, such as Tabs, Reference Desk for writers, and Personas, which allows users to visually customize their browser. Virgin began as a European airline and built a global lifestyle brand. As noted earlier, Virgin is today in music, clothing, mobile, lending, fitness, and space travel. These businesses all contribute some type of asset to the company and brand, and these contributions ebb and flow over time. Virgin has the mojo to attract early customers with its latest, bright V-objects. For Virgin and other companies looking to extend their brands, a network-enabled share platform becomes an opportune way to try out new products.

It's important in any business, but perhaps more so in a Mesh business, to identify the group of people who you think are going to be your early customers. I always look for customers with a high threshold for pain and a robust sense of humor. It's a winning combination for testing new products and building loyal early followers, which everyone needs. And no matter what you think is a compelling offer and the perfect price, the right structure, and the brilliant experience, it's important to understand the customers' point of view. Are your customers less concerned about the cost than they are about the coverage? Some people are willing to pay a form of insurance in case something happens. Suppose they have to go pick up their kid and they have a shared car or bike, and they get there and it's not ready or not well maintained. Is there a concierge service? The question you ask yourself is: Are we as a business in condition to deliver on our promise? We can easily take their money. We're good at that part. What about delivery on the real promise?

As in any business, you must match the expectation of the customer with the offering. Mesh businesses offer a wide range of ways to invite new people in. The access-to-a-product mechanism gives you more choices about how to go to market and engage new customers. You get frequent feedback, even if the message is that no one is buying the story. And matching what customers are ready for today does not mean that you're stuck with this structure or offer forever. The Mesh method allows you to micro-cast opportunities and easily change offers over time. As with any business, structure your business to ensure that you exceed expectations. Early customers will be your word of mouth. They're going to help you build your business and refine your offering. When you're confident that your offer is finely honed for your market, these early adopters will also help you grow through their social networks. This is all classic stuff, but especially true for a Mesh business.

leap out from a base.

As you start to dig in, whether you're focused on single moms, aging parents, young professionals, or musicians, the vitality of the relationship is one of the single biggest assets you're going to have in your business. Make the conversation palpable and interactive in order to build trust. Provoke your market. No one will notice you otherwise. You may annoy, but at least you'll get a reaction. Seek joy and love, of course, but the worst outcome is that no one cares or engages. Your ability to continue an active dialogue, and continually anticipate and act on requests, will give you a huge advantage over any competitive company.

Marketers basically aggregate an audience or a particular like-minded market and speak to them through brand sexiness, or particular offerings, or a price point, or however it is that they think they're making their product or service unique. The first wheel that got sold was that model. An advantage of a Mesh business is that people are often self-identified. Mesh business get lots of information on the way in which people interact with their goods and services. Your customers self-identify by telling you, "I want an electric vehicle," or "I'm willing to give loans to people who are funding their kids' college, but I don't want to give loans to people who are getting out of credit card debt."

be allergic to stagnation.

When people have life changes, such as preparing to have a child or downsizing their home, they often need incremental bursts of material goods. They are often prepared to get rid of things that are no longer useful. Those are interesting moments. As kids go through stages of growth, they change toys, games, equipment, and clothing. Enter clothing swaps, such as peace. love. swap. This service, like the thredUP clothing swap described earlier, is responding to the fact that nobody likes to spend $100 on a pair of pants that is worn twice and then gets thrown out or given away. It's used this opportunity to tap into a community of parents—many of whom are already part of social networks—who buy clothes for kids who grow out of them quickly. Once in the Mesh network, parents can be offered other services. Moms might be a target for car-sharing and bike-sharing businesses that had previously focused primarily on a university crowd.

Two demographics, retiring boomers and young people, are classic targets for a share platform infrastructure. These two groups are likely to be open and interested. Relieving the burdens of ownership, the joy of access, and the favorable trade-off between convenience and cost are all attractive.

When people are getting ready to retire, they may downsize their home, or move from the suburbs to the city. For retiring boomers, the Mesh, particularly the Own-to-Mesh model, may be very attractive. You can help them figure out a way to simplify their lives without losing access to what they need now. You can help them connect to other people, or leverage their budget. The services are often compelling, "right-sized," and secure. For younger people, Mesh businesses will embody the richness of a lifestyle of access to shared goods and services. In this way the Mesh clearly enables sharing when some of the parties may not own a thing. Ownership is not a prerequisite to sharing.

A Mesh business can help retired people spend less money while getting the same quality of life. They also travel—they're looking for lots of experiences, and to cover a lot of terrain without a lot of risk or cost. Since many are living on a fixed income, most of them definitely want lower costs. Maybe they want to stay in their home, but use it as a base camp. Their friends are still there. They identify with the community. They are a ripe market for home sharing and other services.

Likewise, younger people are moving toward medium- or high-density locations. They want a social environment. They want a lot of services, such as bars and pubs, restaurants, and entertainment venues. They can use public transportation to move around a city without having to worry about transporting a child to school or after-school activities. Young people are another prime category for Mesh businesses. Over 70 percent use social network sites. They've got jobs and a social life in the city. They're moving around, doing fun things, being on their own, developing a career and a personal social network.

leverage the "now," grasshopper.

In the start-up world, we say that having very little cash to start a business is often much better than having too much. At the very least, behave and spend as though you have little. Having sufficient capital to start something, but not enough to get into trouble is generally the right balance. You need enough capital so that you're not starving the business. You also need enough capital so that you're not giving a show-a-little-thigh version of your business model to a future competitor who is capitalized when you're not. In that case, you're doing all the hard work only to get beat by a good listener with a bank account.

But if you start to scale up your business and make investments in infrastructure ahead of understanding what's really fundamental—or the important nuances that make your service irresistible—you can waste a whole lot of money. Your business plan is basically a fiction version for the first couple of years. It takes that long to understand the cycles and essentials, who your customers really are, how to retain them, what they're going to value, how they're going to pay you, and why your model is unique. You need time to get into the market, observe how that market is changing, and understand what makes your offer compelling. Give yourself that time.

The capital needed for a Mesh business depends on models. You can choose something that's very capital-intensive, like having to buy the infrastructure for managing fleets of cars. Or you can do something like customizing an existing platform for a clothing swap, toy swap, Own-to-Mesh shared car, shared bike, or home exchange. The other big variable here is geographic reach. In general these businesses have started with a focus in a local urban area. The amount of capital available to you will likely shape how you craft your offer and choose to go to market. For these types of things, the infrastructure—the software and the technology—often exists in a form where you don't have to pay very much. This is referred to as an application service provider, or ASP, model. (A related term is software as a service, or SaaS; it is also sometimes referred to as "services in the cloud.") With ASP, instead of laying out a lot of cash to buy software or to buy computers to run it, you pay as you go.

If you want software that allows you to track home exchanges, there are Web sites that allow you to use the infrastructure they've created. Amazon and other companies offer hosting, Web development, and fulfillment services. They give you access to their hardware, which is run by the same teams of people that set up the infrastructure for the company. Amazon offers not only a hosting service to run your Web site, but also a back end for collecting payments. (As noted, Kickstarter, Etsy, and many other brands, both large and start-up, use the Amazon back end.) You can also use the pick-and-pack facilities of FedEx, UPS, or Amazon, instead of setting up a whole warehouse to receive inventory. These in fact are business-to-business examples of Mesh businesses.

finally, give serendipity a big squeeze.

An important part of any Mesh model is serendipity. Simply put, the frequency of serendipity can increase dramatically in the Mesh. In the past, I might have arrived in Frankfurt, learned that my connecting flight is canceled, and spent four hours in the Frankfurt airport. With a lot of good fortune, I might have run into a colleague who was also "visiting" the airport. But these gemlike moments were rare. In twenty-five years of world travel, I can count them on one hand. Now that we are all carting around mobile devices, and tweeting and checking in on various services, I can easily inform others of my location. Instead of a purely chance encounter, I can use the technology to find any friends or associates who might be nearby in Frankfurt. What was once an unlikely, chance event can now more often be engineered to happen. These tools enhance the quality of my life and work by creating occasions to share time with people who inspire me, engage me, and bring me joy.

In the Mesh, people find incredible surprises that make unexpected things (and people) just stand out. Serendipity can pop in for a visit through partnerships, or the data collected, or new markets reached. Other events to look for and cherish are outspoken and thrilled or disappointed customers, competitors missing the bull's-eye, and new ideas about how to design, value, or price products. These lessons and openings may come from the most surprising of places. The forces that drive the Mesh are on the rise. There is the compelling need to find new efficiencies. There is the expanding capacity of social and Web-based mobile networks. There are the new mapping services and open government and transportation platforms. There is distrust of old brands—and the growing power of consumers to say, and get, what they want. These trends and the technology create more and more delightful new serendipities. As they expand, so will the opportunities for success. Go find 'em. *Buena suerte*.

Epilogue to the Paperback Edition

> 75% of the world's population will be living in cities by the year 2050.
>
> —The Urban Age Project

> A pessimist sees the difficulty in every opportunity; an optimist sees the opportunity in every difficulty.
>
> —Winston Churchill

Since *The Mesh* was first published in 2010, the Sharing Economy has moved from a quiet purr to a global attention-grabbing roar. Thousands of new ventures have launched, providing customers access to an array of experiences or goods rather than simply selling one product at a time. Additionally, well-heeled corporate giants like American Express, Apple, Barclays, BMW, Choice, Ford, GM, GE, Osklen, Tesco, Unilever, and many others are boldly exploring innovative ways to create teams, partnerships, brands, products, and test new markets. These companies know that "shared" offerings now thrive in lieu of the previously adored traditional product sales model. Not surprisingly, with the smell and shine of new opportunities emerging, private and public investors have enriched their holdings in companies building community-based marketplaces. Many are also bringing their own Midas touch to data in a world where access increasingly triumphs over ownership.

Many of the companies discussed in this book have ramped up impressively over the past year. For example, Crushpad raised additional capital to expand and refine its offerings. It launched Crushpad Syndicate, a crowd-funding model where wine enthusiasts can create a brand and share the cost and returns (some very liquid), with "peer" investors.

ThredUP, a venture capital funded startup that has created a marketplace for children's "gently used" clothing, functioning similarly to Netflix or Lovefilm, is also adjusting its model and approach. Additionally, there are similar services popping up in Brazil with BoxKids and KidsKarton in Germany. While its primary offering remains the same, thredUP is a strong example of a community-driven mesh business. As a marketplace, the dynamics of the supply side (in this case, gently used clothing to be sold) being rightly balanced by the demand side (customers seeking a particular size or type of clothing) requires regular observation, support, and even incentives ensuring the ecosystem has the essential ingredients to sustain and grow. In one moment, after examining community data, it was clear that new clothing listed on the service would get snapped up within twenty-four hours. While this shows enthusiasm and serious engagement on the part of their marketplace, the management team realized that this would create a less than perfect shopping experience for first-time customers. Several new programs were introduced including one that paid existing customers "low supply credits" to list items in high demand at low supply. As with any ecosystem, thredUP created a balance necessary to make a two-sided marketplace thrive and grow. Its community will continue to function as a microeconomy issuing new forms of currency to maintain a healthy level of growth and engagement.

Kickstarter has inspired artists, "makers," farmers, product developers, and entrepreneurs, and similar services have been created in such far flung locales as Brazil with Catarse, Movere. me, incentivador, benfeitoria, and impulse, and in Sweden with fundedbyme.com. Kickstarter and Kisskissbankbank in France have spurred a "dreams to reality" service for various projects and companies. Two examples of projects that received donations in excess of their monetary goals are "exposition echoes," a contemporary art installation in Paris at the Musée Nissim de Camondo, and TikTok, an iPod nano wristwatch, which aimed to raise $15,000 for its first production run but actually raised $960,000 and is now carried by top retailers including Apple. This demonstrates how Mesh companies with a self-sustaining business model provide an in-market product test that can later be successfully leveraged efficiently through partnerships. This process provides more benefit to the creator and their community while generating much less waste.

On a personal note, I have had the privilege of meeting and working with many people from diverse backgrounds, cultures, interests, and concerns as I've had the opportunity to share my Mesh-based views and experiences. I've also listened to their thoughts and experiences, which is actually of greater interest to me. As a global community, we are certainly at an inflection point. From the perspective of the Mesh or Sharing Economy, there are **two** core and fundamental opportunities on our horizon.

First, we, as a global community, have so many resources, talent, and capacity that so often go untapped. Our big opportunity is to refine our ability to make the most of what we already have; in other words, maximize yield management. This has a significant benefit across industries, within large enterprises and, perhaps most urgently, within and between our communities and cities. Cities thrive when they act as a platform for inviting mesh businesses and ecosystems.

These business models focus on getting more value from what already exists. For example, Loosecubes, a global network of office desks or *cubes*, operates where there is an excess capacity of space, creating a ready work community in exchange for talent, money, or another currency. Buzzcar, a service in France much like RelayRides and WhipCar, allows you to rent your neighbor's available car. It comes as no surprise that this business was founded by Robin Chase, the cofounder of Zipcar.

Second, trust is on the wane. Governments and big corporations have revealed their agenda of winning at our expense. But big doesn't necessarily mean reliable or good anymore. At the same time, we may just as easily trust our neighbors and friends. Companies like Etsy, Zipcar, bici, super marmite, Zazcar, Carrotmob, Solar Mosaic, Vayable, Frents, OhSoWe, icancanu, Aqush, and many other peer-to-peer marketplaces depend on people trusting their peers with their things.

Do you?

We are participating in the birth of a new social operating system. To function dynamically will require that the way we have evaluated one another, validated claims, and determined who and what to vouch for is compatible with the increasing pulse of our peer to peer, share-based connections. We are shifting away from managing a debt-based economy. We are slowly re-learning to dole out the currency of trust of, by, and for our peers in an access driven ecosystem. This nuanced dance will continue to evolve between companies, investors, policy makers, and the communities they depend upon and serve. New metrics, scorekeepers, clarity, and rules of engagement are required. These, like most things in our world, will be introduced, tested, and tweaked as necessary to work harmoniously in each community and culture. Then they will be able to work at scale.

Early though it may be in the evolution of the Mesh, there have already been several good examples of what types of human conduct will drive our access score up or down. Not surprisingly, the happy path to a high trust access score arises from a respect for others and their things. This translates simply to returning products on time and in the same or better condition than when you found it. This includes disclosing disrepair, malfunction, or loss, especially if it happened on your watch. As the quality of our lives becomes increasingly dependent on our access score, this new currency will be challenged, validated, and, of course, gamed. New standards, agencies, and operating systems will be proposed, revised, and asserted. In the meantime, those of us who are creating ventures or participating in share-based marketplaces would be wise to liberally share our lessons learned. In this way, we will reduce the expensive waste of repeating mistakes. Errors come at a high cost to our balance sheets, brand equity, environment, and of course, the hard-won trust of our peers and customers.

Earth is the mother of all share platforms. Our continued success depends on our embracing this reality. We are undeniably connected—to each other, to our communities, to our things, and to nature.

Further delay in embracing our connections will come at an exorbitant cost.

Creative Commons License

You are free to Share—to copy, distribute, and transmit—the following Mesh Directory under the following conditions:

- **Attribution**—You must attribute the work in the manner specified by the author or licensor (but not in any way that suggests that they endorse you or your use of the work):

- **No Derivative Works**—You may not alter, transform, or build upon this work.

With the understanding that:

- **Waiver**—Any of the above conditions can be waived if you get permission from the copyright holder.

- **Other Rights**—In no way are any of the following rights affected by the license:
  - Your fair dealing or fair use rights;
  - The author's moral rights;
  - Rights other persons may have either in the work itself or in how the work is used, such as publicity or privacy rights.

- **Notice**—For any reuse or distribution, you must make clear to others the license terms of this work.

The Mesh Directory

The full, community updated directory of over 1,000 Mesh ventures is available online at www.meshing.it. In the pages that follow you will find an abridged listing of Mesh ventures in finance, fashion, real estate, food and wine, energy, technology, gardening, transportation, home improvement, and many other categories. Each section begins with a brief description of how the highlighted businesses leverage the power of the Mesh to make access to goods and services superior to owning them. In addition, one Mesh venture per category is described in even greater detail. The directory is meant to showcase the breadth of possibility in the Mesh, to give a sense of the type of business models that are in the market today, and to blatantly encourage exploration. Does your company, organization, or business-yet-to-be belong here?

ACCESSORIES AND GIFTS

Mesh companies that offer accessories and gifts are a great way for consumers to enjoy a variety of new merchandise, without the burden of ownership, through rentals, swaps, and gift card exchanges. Jewelry rental companies, for instance, give fashionistas the opportunity to wear rare gems for a fraction of their selling price. Accessory-trading platforms enable members to acquire "new" goods in exchange for gently used jewelry and beauty products. Other companies trade unwanted gift cards for cash or swap them for gift cards redeemable at the consumer's preferred companies.

Who says you can't be both chic and practical in today's financial climate? Not Adorn. A pioneer in the jewelry rental business, Adorn helps people glam up for special events and stay within budget. They give customers the opportunity to enjoy a range of accessories for all occasions without emptying their savings on one highly prized, but seldom worn piece. To gain access to Adorn's Meshy jewelry, people must first sign up for a free membership. Customers then identify jewelry they want to rent and check its availability for their preferred date of delivery. Adorn guarantees the jewelry will arrive via UPS two days before the day of a special event and provides a prepaid envelope for its return. Best of all, the jewelry is insured from the moment it leaves Adorn until the moment it returns.

Adorn: Diamond jewelry rentals for special occasions.
http://www.adorn.com

Avelle: Authentic designer handbag, jewelry, sunglasses, and watch rentals.
http://www.bagborroworsteal.com

Beehive Co-op: Handmade products from emerging designers.
http://www.beehiveco-op.com

Buy1Give1: B1G1 lets you see the tangible impact that your generosity has on people.
http://www.b1g1.com

Exboyfriend Jewelry: Trade platform for jewelry gifted by an ex. Users blog the story of their jewelry.
http://www.exboyfriendjewelry.com

15Gifts: Makes gift-giving easy by removing the decision process.
http://www.15gifts.com

Gift Card Rescue: Gift card exchange service.
http://www.giftcardrescue.com

Handbag Hire HQ: Designer handbag hires.
http://www.handbaghirehq.co.uk

MakeupAlley: Online beauty product swap.
http://www.makeupalley.com

Swapagift: Gift card exchange.
http://www.swapagift.com

ARTS AND CRAFTS

Art-centered Mesh businesses provide customers with convenient, less expensive alternatives to the traditional ownership model, and they continually seek ways to improve and expand their offerings. Companies may rent original art to both private and commercial consumers by allowing them to select pieces for framing and installation. Alternatively, Mesh businesses in this category may create physical or virtual space, such as an online forum, for communities of artists to form and celebrate their mediums through conversation.

There are many other fresh, art-centered business models waiting to be developed and brought to the Mesh. Take

Carbonmade. In December 2005, Dave Gorum perceived a common need shared by many artists for an easy way to manage an online portfolio. After successfully coding a platform for himself and a few designer friends, Gorum soon invited the public to join Carbonmade. The site allows artists to showcase their artwork in online portfolios with the use of simple tools. It offers two flavors of membership: Meh., which is free, and Whoo!, which costs $12 per month. So how exactly is Carbonmade different? By mitigating the pain of manually updating a portfolio, it allows users to focus solely on displaying their art.

99%: Research arm of Behance, a company dedicated to bringing creative ideas to fruition.
http://www.the99percent.com

Art Rent & Lease: Artwork rentals and leases.
http://www.artrentandlease.com

Art.sy: A new way to discover art that you'll love.
http://art.sy

Craftworks: Craftworks is an artisan cooperative that features the work of over 75 crafters.
http://www.craftworkscoop.com

The Intersection: A San Francisco art space that presents new and experimental work in the fields of literature, theater, music, and the visual arts.
http://www.theintersection.org

Open Design: Open-source design firm that aims to close the creativity gap between product design and other fields (music, graphic design, animation, and photography).
http://www.ronen-kadushin.com/Open_Design.asp

Prop Art New York: Original modern art rentals for commercial or private space.
http://www.modernartforrent.com

Spoonflower: Community of textile artists.
http://www.spoonflower.com

Trust Art: Social platform that commissions public artworks.
http://trustart.org

World Artist Exchange: Facilitates global travel and community among a network of artists.
http://www.worldartistexchange.ning.com

BOOKS AND WRITING

In this category, Mesh businesses aim to keep books circulating among readers by enabling social networks of literary enthusiasts to rent and swap books and exchange reading recommendations. Book-swap companies give bookworms an opportunity to replace their old titles for "new" ones by swapping with other members. Swaps are generally managed by a system where members earn and spend points while swapping, or a direct swap system where members arrange book-for-book swaps. Book- and writing-centered social networks enable members to engage in a variety of activities, including discussions about creative writing and dating services for book lovers.

BookMooch is a used-book exchange platform that operates on a point-based system. Members first earn a percentage of a point by listing a book they're willing to swap. Additional points are earned by giving books away and can be spent by requesting a book from someone else. Driven by a frustration with the limited availability of certain books in multiple countries, Book-Mooch founder John Buckman devised a special point system for overseas book swaps. The company also gives members the option to donate their points to charities or children's hospitals whose patients would enjoy a good read. Another perk of joining BookMooch: membership is free. Moochers are only responsible for shipping costs.

BookCrossing: Members register books with BookCrossing, leave them in public spaces, then track their journeys around the globe.
http://www.bookcrossing.com

Booking Authors: Booking Authors is an independent, niche marketing and PR business for book authors and experts seeking influential, community-building speaking engagements.
http://www.bookingauthors.com

BookMesh: Lets you connect with local book lovers with similar taste.
http://bookmesh.com

BookMooch: Point-based book-exchange system. Earn a point by giving someone a book, and spend it by requesting a book from someone else.
http://www.bookmooch.com

Chegg: Textbook rentals.
http://www.chegg.com

dpr-barcelona: A publishing company specializing in high quality architecture and design books.
http://www.dpr-barcelona.com

Goodreads: Social networking site where readers recommend books, compare what they're reading, keep track of what they've read, and form book clubs.
http://www.goodreads.com

Night Owl's Press: A boutique consulting firm of print and media experts.
http://www.nightowlspress.com

Penguin Dating: Dating service for book lovers.
http://penguin.match.com

Readeo: Readeo lets friends and family read stories together no matter how far apart they are.
http://www.readeo.com

Text4Swap: Book-for-book swapping system for students to exchange used textbooks.
http://www.text4swap.com

The Montague Bookmill: Used bookstore north of Amherst, Massachusetts.
http://www.montaguebookmill.com

CLOTHING SWAP

Clothing-centered Mesh businesses make it fun and easy to refresh an outdated wardrobe without purchasing new clothing. They host fun clothes swaps or make it easy to exchange duds through online platforms for small membership fees. Some offer designer clothing rentals, while others provide online platforms for fashion-loving communities to design and create "new" clothes made from recycled materials.

Fashion-conscious women may continue to go gaga over the latest styles, but many are gaining an awareness of the inevitable environmental toll of buying new clothing. So what's a girl to do? The London-based company Swishing has an answer: "Rustle clothes from friends." Women are now throwing Swishing parties across the globe—in the U.K., China, South Africa, Brazil, and the United States—to trade gently used, fashionable clothing. All attendees bring at least one article of clothing and take what they like once the swish opens. You can also throw your own Swishing party by visiting the Web site, registering, and adding an event. For the trend spotters among us: Swishing is the new pink.

The Clothing Exchange: The Clothing Exchange is a professional swapping service that promotes the simple notion of swapping instead of shopping for a better wardrobe and better world.
http://www.clothingexchange.com.au

Clothing Swap: Coordinates clothing swaps across the country.
http://www.clothingswap.com

Dig 'N' Swap: Dig 'N' Swap is a way to swap fashionable clothing and accessories with people who share your passion for fashion.
http://www.dignswap.com

Fabricly: Online crowdsourced fashion designs produced just for you.
http://www.fabricly.com

Girl Meets Dress: Girl Meets Dress is an online boutique where you can borrow the latest designer dresses.
http://www.girlmeetsdress.com

Golden Hook: Customers design their own hats and then choose the grandmothers they want to knit them.
http://www.goldenhook.fr

ModCloth: Consumers become virtual fashion buyers and help ModCloth choose which clothing designs get created.
http://www.modcloth.com

Rent the Runway: Designer clothing rentals.
http://www.renttherunway.com

Swishing: Clothing swap parties.
http://www.swishing.com

Threadless: Community-centered apparel store that allows members to submit T-shirt designs online. The designs are put to a public vote, and a small percentage are selected for printing and retail.
http://www.threadless.com

ThredUP: Online platform for swapping kids clothes and toys.
http://www.thredup.com

CO-OPS AND GENERAL COMMUNITY

Mesh businesses build communities by uniting individuals who share common interests. Using information technology, they organize social networks and create opportunities for collaboration. These community-centered businesses support groups of all stripes, including moms, foodies, dairy farmers, babysitters, college kids, consumers, auto enthusiasts, and more.

Every day, a Chicago-based company called Groupon features a deal on the best stuff to eat, see, do, and buy in cities across the United States. Its strategy: collective buying power. By leveraging the power of group purchasing and promising businesses a minimum number of customers, Groupon can offer discounts on popular goods and services. To purchase a deal, members click the "buy" button before the offer ends at midnight. If the minimum number of people sign up, Groupon will charge your card and send a link to your Groupon. No one will be charged if the minimum required number of buyers is not met.

BioCurious: BioCurious is a new biology collaborative lab space where citizen science moves out of the classroom and into the community.
http://biocuriosity.wordpress.com

Bright Neighbor: Bright Neighbor combines community involvement and social tools to help local governments and communities increase livability and sustainability.
http://www.brightneighbor.com

CEOs for Cities: Network of urban leaders dedicated to building and sustaining the next generation of cities.
http://www.ceosforcities.org

Cooperatives Europe: Promotes the co-op model for sustainable economic progress with social objectives.
http://www.coopseurope.coop

Food Front Cooperative: A community grocery store in Portland, OR.
http://www.foodfront.coop

Get Satisfaction: Gets customers and employees working together to openly improve the way help is delivered.
http://getsatisfaction.com

Hunch: Based on the collective knowledge of the community, Hunch offers recommendations to address your personal challenges or need for advice.
http://www.hunch.com

InnoCentive: A Web-based community that matches scientists with research and development challenges presented by companies worldwide.
http://www.innocentive.com

Just Coffee Cooperative: Just Coffee Cooperative is a worker-owned coffee roaster dedicated to creating and expanding a model of trade based on transparency, equality, and human dignity.
http://www.justcoffee.coop

Local Agricultural Community Exchange: Commons for Vermont family farmers and their communities to exchange information and celebrate food.
http://www.lacevt.org

Mama Bake: A community of mothers who share the responsiblities of cooking.
http://mamabake.com

NeighborGoods: Online community where neighbors share stuff.
http://neighborgoods.net

Siouxland Energy and Livestock Cooperative: Adds value to producer-member corn through least-cost ethanol production.
http://www.siouxlandenergy.com

UpMyStreet: Helps users choose new places to live, save time and money in and around their homes, and find local services.
http://www.upmystreet.com

EDUCATION

Information technology is crucial for providing access to quality education. Mesh organizations in this category use it to deliver educational solutions to underprivileged students, online classes, and others who simply want to learn. Some organizations develop programs that teach specific subjects such as writing, science, technology, or engineering. Others aim to raise awareness about the social and economic inequalities facing schools and teachers in the United States.

In 2007, five cofounders launched a social learning network that connects people who can teach with people who want to learn. They call it the School of Everything (SoE). And it's true: from biology to beekeeping, history to hula hooping, SoE has got it all. Whether you live in France, Germany, India, Mexico, or Canada, the SoE Web site will help you contact other members and meet up to share knowledge and learn new things. SoE's services are 100 percent free.

826 Valencia: Volunteer-based writing program dedicated to supporting students ages six to eighteen in San Francisco.
http://www.826valencia.org

iLoveSchools.com: Raises awareness of classroom resource inequalities facing schools and teachers in the United States.
http://www.iloveschools.com

Insead: Brings people, cultures, and ideas together to transform organizations through management education.
http://www.insead.edu

Livemocha: Online language program and language learning community.
http://www.livemocha.com

National Lab Day: Initiative to build local communities that foster collaboration among volunteers, students, and educators.
http://www.nationallabday.org

The Oxbox School: The Oxbow School is an interdisciplinary semester program for high school students to strengthen their abilities in creative and critical inquiry by combining rigorous studio art proactive with innovative academics.
http://www.oxbowschool.org

P2PU: Online community of open study groups for short university courses.
http://p2pu.org

Rayku: A p2p tutoring site for college and university students to get help on demand.
http://www.rayku.com

School of Everything: Helps people learn or teach whatever, whenever, and wherever they want by connecting them with other members of the community.
http://www.schoolofeverything.com

TEC The Education Cooperative: Delivers educational solutions to suburban communities west of Boston.
http://www.tec-coop.org

ENERGY

Mesh organizations commonly form cooperatives to deliver energy to member-owners. Energy cooperatives are voluntary organizations, open to all individuals who are willing to accept the responsibilities of membership. They operate under democratic member control and require equal economic participation from each member-owner. As a result of their group buying power, cooperatives can offer significant savings on the cost of energy to their members. Additionally, they often promote the use of alternative or sustainable energy to improve the quality of life in the areas they serve. In this category, you'll find energy providers from around the world that operate under a cooperative ethos.

Over the course of a year, one 600-kilowatt wind turbine will produce enough energy to power an average of 450 homes. In 2004, Westmill Wind Farm Co-operative became the first energy producer in southern England to connect turbines to an on-site substation where electricity is metered and sold. Locals were given the first opportunity to invest in the farm's renewable energy, but by 2008, commercial generation was under way. The co-op now serves over 2,300 members and averts more than 5,000 metric tons of carbon dioxide per year. Westmill Wind Farm welcomes new members who want to learn about wind as a renewable energy.

Ag Energy Co-operative: Canada's largest farm energy cooperative.
http://www.agenergy.coop

Clean Cities: Organizes a network of volunteer coalitions that promote alternative fuels and hybrid vehicles.
http://www1.eere.energy.gov/cleancities

Community Wind: Empowers communities to develop and own wind energy.
http://www.windustry.org/communitywind

Co-op Power: Promotes a sustainable energy future.
http://www.cooppower.coop

Dairyland Power Cooperative: Generation and transmission cooperative based in Wisconsin.
http://www.dairynet.com

Middlegrunden Wind Turbine Co-operative: Cooperative offshore wind farm in Copenhagen.
http://www.middelgrunden.dk

Peace Energy Cooperative: Member-run co-op that delivers renewable energy to residents in British Columbia.
http://www.peaceenergy.ca

Soar Energy: Member-owned solar and renewable energy buyers' cooperative.
http://www.soarenergy.org

Sydney Energy Cooperative: Aims to involve Sydney, Australia, in sustainable energy-related activities.
http://www.energycoop.com.au

Touchstone Energy Cooperatives: Represents a nationwide alliance made up of consumer-owned electric co-ops in forty-six states.
https://touchstoneenergy.cooperative.com

Windunie: Group of Dutch wind turbine owners who feed sustainable energy into the grid for consumers to purchase.
http://www.windunie.nl

FINANCIAL CURRENCY

Mesh companies in the financial sector offer lucrative alternatives for borrowers, lenders, investors, and others who enter traditional financial relationships. Peer-to-peer (p2p) lending marketplaces, for instance, enable people to lend and borrow money with each other while sidestepping banks. Through social lending, both lenders and borrowers get better rates than in the traditional banking model. Bartering for goods and services is another alternative financial transaction gaining popularity among consumers.

In the wake of the global social networking phenomena, social lending is starting to ramp up: p2p lending marketplaces have sprouted in Japan, Australia, the United States, Italy, and the Netherlands. In 2007 Germany added itself to the list when a company called smava joined the ranks of Internet-enabled social lending platforms. Think of it as borrowing and lending from your family and friends, except that there are thousands of people who are ready to meet your terms. After registering for a free membership and undergoing credit checks, German residents can lend or request a loan through smava's online platform. Borrowers post a request ranging from 500 to 10,000 euros, describe how they will use the money, and indicate their preferred interest rate. Lenders then bid on the loans in multiples of 500 euros. The company charges the borrower a fee totaling 1 percent of the loan amount.

BigCarrot: Facilitates social lending. Individuals loan money to businesses in Britain.
http://www.bigcarrot.com

Booper: A p2p lending platform in Italy.
https://www.booper.it

Community Connect Trade Association: Association of business owners and professionals who trade their products and services for things they need.
http://www.communityconnecttrade.com

Expensure: Simplifies the complexity of sharing bills and expenses with other people.
http://expensure.com

GrupoBarter: Facilitates barter in South America.
http://www.grupobarter.com

Kisskissbankbank: Tool that helps artists and production companies fund their projects.
http://www.kisskissbankbank.com

Lending Club: Social lending network that unites investors and borrowers to provide personal loans.
http://www.lendingclub.com

New Resource Bank: New Resource Bank supports people, organizations, and companies that strive for an environmental and social return as well as a financial return.
https://www.newresourcebank.com

Outvesting: Members commit money to businesses and expect nothing in return.
http://www.outvesting.org

People Capital: Allows students to lend and borrow based on their academic merit.
http://www.people2capital.com

Pro Mujer: Women's development and microfinance organization.
https://promujer.org

Rabobank Group: Financial cooperative based in the Netherlands.
http://www.rabobankamerica.com

SecondMarket: Marketplace and auction platform for illiquid assets.
http://www.secondmarket.com

smava: Online p2p lending marketplace based in Germany.
http://www.smava.de

SuperRewards: Enables social publishers to turn virtual economies into real revenue.
http://www.srpoints.com

The Receivables Exchange: Allows businesses to sell receivables to institutional investors in exchange for working capital.
http://www.receivablesxchange.com

Zopa: Marketplace for social lending. People lend and borrow money with each other while sidestepping banks.
http://us.zopa.com

FOOD, WINE, AND BEER

Food-, wine-, and beer-centered Mesh businesses give consumers access to unique, community-oriented food products and services. Member-owned cooperative food stores offer discounts on natural food to members who work in exchange for membership benefits. Through outreach and events, food co-ops offer additional resources including education about nutrition, food safety, health, and community issues. Other Mesh companies in this category help customers blend, label, and sell custom-made wine, form cooking clubs, and connect with other food enthusiasts.

Can one meal help rebuild a nation's communities? It can. One Sunday in July 2009, nearly 1 million Brits shared lunch on their lawns and in their streets. Appropriately dubbed The Big Lunch, the event was an opportunity for neighborhood residents to break bread and share stories in an effort to begin rebuilding Britain's communities. It was a hit. Now, what was once just a big idea has turned into an annual event: more lunching is in the works.

Bake Club: Provides directions for creating a cooking club and tools to manage it.
http://www.bakeclub.co.uk

Belize Fishermen Cooperative Association: Fosters cooperation among member cooperatives.
http://www.bfca.bz

BoozeMonkey: Social network for lovers of Australian and New Zealand wine.
http://www.boozemonkey.com

Boston Food Swap: An outlet for sharing surplus goods and offer an alternative to store-bought items, helping swappers eat locally, sustainably, and affordably.
http://www.bostonfoodswap.com

Brooklyn Brew Shop: The Brooklyn Brew Shop helps people make really good beer from really good ingredients by selling kits, mixes, and everything else at the Brooklyn Flea on weekends and online to the rest of the world.
http://brooklynbrewshop.com

City Winery: New York City winery where people make wine and meet new friends.
http://www.citywinery.com

Local Dirt: Helps consumers buy, sell, and find local food.
http://www.localdirt.com

Outstanding in the Field: Celebrates food at the source.
http://www.outstandinginthefield.com

Oven Alley: Allows people to buy and sell homemade dishes.
http://ovenally.com

The Big Lunch: Once a year, people in the U.K. sit down to lunch with their neighbors—a simple but profound act of community.
http://www.thebiglunch.com

GARDENING

As people flock to dense urban areas, many are challenged by the prospect of growing their own food without ample land for gardening. Mesh businesses offer a possible solution by connecting landless gardeners to homeowners with unused plots that are ripe for land sharing. Other Mesh businesses in this category arrange seed and vegetable swaps through online exchange platforms.

In early 2009, an organization called Landshare observed an excess of underused or forgotten land in the U.K. It soon realized that some of it could be cultivated for vegetables and fruit. So Landshare set out to connect would-be growers with people who have available land, uniting those in the U.K. who have a passion for homegrown food. To "get growing," Landshare helps you create a profile, post a listing that states where you are and what you have to offer, and get connected. Since Landshare's launch in April 2009, nearly 50,000 members have already signed on.

Farmbook: Farmbook is a free exchange for farmers and others to buy and sell agricultural goods, raw materials, equipment, livestock, services, and much more.
http://www.farmbook.info

Folia: Folia is an online social garden tracking app that lets you track, journal, and share the progress of your plants and gardens.
http://myfolia.com

Landshare: Online platform where landowners, growers, or helpers can advertise their offerings.
http://www.landshare.net

Pie Ranch: Pie Ranch helps rural and urban people understand the source of their food, and to work together to bring greater health to the food system from seed to table.
http://www.pieranch.org

Seedy People: Online seed swap.
http://seedypeople.co.uk

SharedEarth: SharedEarth aims to build a broad and trusting community of land owners and gardeners that yields the efficient use of land and a greener planet.
http://www.sharedearth.com

Urban Garden Share: Matches homeowners with unused garden space to gardeners.
http://www.urbangardenshare.org

Wasatch Community Gardens: Empowers people in Salt Lake City, Utah, to grow and eat healthy, organic, local food.
http://wasatchgardens.org

WWOOF: Worldwide network that links people who want to volunteer on organic farms with people who are looking for volunteer help.
http://wwoof.org

yours2share: Provides information about landsharing.
http://www.yours2share.com/fractional-info/landshare.shtml

GOODS SWAP

Mesh businesses reduce the stress that buy-and-throw-away companies exert on natural resources by keeping usable goods in circulation. Goods swaps or barter exchange platforms enable consumers to trade unwanted goods or services for those they do want. While some platforms encourage direct, good-for-good swaps, others are managed by point systems. Free classified listings enable community members to arrange and negotiate trades among themselves as well.

Kashless is a new kind of marketplace where everything is free. Its goal is to connect those who want to give things away with those who are looking for gently used, free stuff. From antique furniture to barbeques, dirt to mealworms, Kashless listings never stop surprising, or delighting, members of the marketplace. Kashless members can browse listings in over 110 U.S. metro areas by neighborhood or category and receive a tax deduction after contributing any free item to the site. In providing an advanced, modern ecommerce platform for reuse, Kashless extends the useful life of products, diverts usable material from entering the waste stream, encourages local consumption, and reduces raw material resource demand.

Bid & Borrow: Online platform for borrowing goods and services.
http://www.bidandborrow.com

DoneDeal: Online classifieds for individuals in Ireland to list goods for sale or trade.
http://www.donedeal.ie

GoSwap: Online platform for home, land, business, yacht, and vehicle exchanges.
http://goswap.org

Quikr: Free local online classifieds. Based in India.
http://www.quikr.com

Return My Pants: A service that lets you track the things you lend and borrow.
http://returnmypants.com

Share Some Sugar: Helps members connect with neighbors who are willing to lend things.
http://www.sharesomesugar.com

Swapit: Online swapping community for young people in the U.K.
http://www.swapit.co.uk

Tausch Ticket: Trading platform for books, movies, music, and games based in Germany.
http://www.tauschticket.de

Toolzdo: Community-building platform that helps users rent, borrow, and swap goods.
http://www.toolzdo.com

urbanMamas: Used outdoor gear exchange for women.
http://www.urbanmamas.com/exchange/outdoor_gear/

HEALTH AND FITNESS

Mesh organizations that offer health and fitness programs focus on how to leverage the power of community to deliver benefits to members. Cooperative health insurance providers, for instance, use their group buying power to help members get the coverage they need at an affordable price. Members of community sports clubs gain access to both scheduled group exercise and a variety of other events through the clubs' social networks.

Aire is an urban performance cooperative of highly experienced athletic and wellness experts who help members accomplish their fitness-related goals. The San Diego–based co-op offers private and group Pilates, cycling, rowing, and TRX classes, as well as access to personal trainers. And as a testament to its community ethos, Aire does not require a membership fee. Instead, members pay Aire trainers directly for their instruction and classes.

Body Mechanix Fitness Cooperative: Fitness co-op in California's San Francisco Bay Area.
http://www.bodymechanixs.com

Community Pharmacy: Workers' cooperative that promotes health in Madison, Wisconsin.
http://www.communitypharmacy.coop

Farmers' Health Cooperative of Wisconsin: Provides farmers and agribusiness with health-care coverage.
http://www.farmershealthcooperative.com

Fitocracy: Fitocracy turns fitness into a game to help users improve their fitness while having more fun at the same time.
http://www.fitocracy.com

Freewheelers of Spartanburg Inc.: Member-based community service organization that promotes bicycle safety.
http://www.freewheelers.info

Growing Green Co-op: Member-based, holistic health education and resource center in Hartford, Connecticut.
http://www.growinggreenevents.com

Knickerbikers: Bicycle touring club based in San Diego, California.
http://www.knickerbikers.com

Patients Like Me: Connects patients with similar life changing conditions.
http://www.patientslikeme.com

row2k: Provides rowing information online.
http://www.row2k.com

Welcome to Recess: Member-based community offering wellness tips and education to local families.
http://www.recessurbanrecreation.com

West Wireless Health Institute: Promotes the use of innovative and cost-effective wireless solutions to meet community needs.
http://www.westwirelesshealth.org

HOBBIES

Mesh organizations can engage anyone who has a hobby—even dollhouse enthusiasts—by providing online exchange platforms where members trade hobby-related tools and information and form niche communities. In this category, Mesh organizations offer services to guitar owners, gamers, sailors, knitters, motorcycle enthusiasts, swingers, and more.

Have you ever seen a nifty thingamajig and wondered how to make it? Instructables might have the answer. It's a Web-based documentation platform where people share what they do and how they do it. For example, one member gives instructions for making a yummy fire-breathing dragon cake using yellow frosting, fruit gems, chocolate covered graham crackers, Fruit Roll-Ups, two nine-inch cakes, and wooden skewers. An Instructables membership will allow you to publish your own instructable (a step-by-step description of something you want to share), vote in contests, keep a member profile, and participate in community forums. Another key benefit of membership is the ability to leave comments on other instructables. It's a great way to ask questions, give praise, or offer improvements to other members of the DIY community.

AllPeopleQuilt: Home of American patchwork and quilting.
http://www.allpeoplequilt.com

BurdaStyle: Bringing the craft of sewing to a new generation of designers, hobbyists, DIYers, and anyone looking to sew.
http://www.burdastyle.com

Crash Space: Community of hackers, artists, makers, and programmers who make things and share space, equipment, and ideas.
http://www.crashspace.org

European Fly Fishing Association: Education in Fly Casting, Fly Fishing, Fly Tying, and Conservation.
http://www.effa.info

Full Throttle Club: Allows members to purchase part ownership of a boat or RV.
http://www.fullthrottleclub.com

Goozex: Trading community for video games and movies.
http://www.goozex.com

Instructables: Web-based documentation platform where people share what they make and how they do it.
http://www.instructables.com

Minkha: Cooperative knitting group.
http://www.minkhasweaters.com

OpenRoadJourney: Community of motorcycle enthusiasts.
http://www.openroadjourney.com

Sail Time: Fractional sailing and boating in North America.
http://www.sailtime.com

HOME IMPROVEMENT

Imagine gaining access to a community toolshed. The need for owning cumbersome or seldom-used tools would disappear, and you would no longer face the burden of maintenance and storage. What's more, the act of sharing would help reduce consumption of raw materials. Mesh organizations in this category aim to make access to landscaping and home repair tools superior to ownership by creating viable share platforms. A "tool library," for instance, lends tools to community members and gives them the advice they need to complete home improvement projects. Membership is generally free, although a small annual dues may be charged. Other Mesh businesses in this category use online platforms to enable tool sharing and swaps among neighbors.

In 2004, four Portland residents founded the North Portland Tool Library (NPTL), a community resource that gives residents access to tools and the know-how required to use them. Its current inventory of five hundred tools includes hammers, saws, ladders, sanders, drills, tampers, tillers, and more. Among the primary goals of the NPTL is to help reduce the cost of maintaining and improving the places community members use to live, work, and play. To that end, the NPTL offers free membership and sponsors free, hands-on workshops to help community members learn to use tools more effectively.

Friends of the Earth: Share tools and DIY equipment with neighbors, friends, or family.
http://www.foe.co.uk/living/tips/swap_tools.html

iFixit: Online step-by-step repair guides that users can use, write, and/or edit.
http://www.ifixit.com

North Portland Tool Library (NPTL): Loans tools to community members for free.
http://northportlandtoollibrary.org

Rebuilding Together Central Ohio Tool Library: Tool library in Columbus, Ohio.
http://www.rtcentralohio.org/toollibrary.htm

Santa Rosa Tool Library: Offers tools for home repair, landscaping, and automotive work for free.
http://borrowtools.org

ToolSwap—USA: Hosts events in California exclusively for swapping tools.
http://www.toolswapusa.com

West Philly Tool Library: Loans tools to community
members for a small yearly fee.
http://westphillytools.org

HUMANITARIAN PROJECTS

Through systems-level design thinking and open-source sharing, Mesh organizations enable teams of professionals to deliver
timely solutions that make lasting differences in underrepre-
sented communities. Some organizations use design to create
socially responsible and environmentally sustainable built environments. Others use the Web as a tool for connecting volunteers
to humanitarian projects and for providing financial assistance
to communities in need.

One in seven people live in slum settlements. By 2020 it will be one in three.
Architecture for Humanity (AfH) displays this unsettling sta-
tistic at the top of its Web page as a call to action. And it's been
largely successful. Since its inception in 1999, the design services
firm has built a global network of more than 40,000 professionals who lend their time and expertise to help bring design,
construction, and development services to communities in need.
From conception to completion, AfH manages all aspects of the
design and construction process to create structures that directly
benefit 10,000 people each year. AfH recently finished construction on Africa's first rural health telecenter, located in Ipuli, Tan-
zania. This project, among others, is a testament to the ability
of AfH to bring people together to build safer, more sustainable,
and more innovative structures.

Acumen Fund: Dissolving poverty through business
innovations and partnerships.
www.acumenfund.org

Architecture for Humanity: Nonprofit design firm that donates services to communities in need.
http://www.architectureforhumanity.org

Catapult Design: Develops and implements human-centered products to help people in need.
http://catapultdesign.org

Design that Matters: Creates new products that allow socially responsible organizations in developing countries to offer improved services.
http://www.designthatmatters.org

FeelGood World: FeelGood is a youth-led nonprofit working to end world hunger "one grilled cheese at a time."
www.feelgoodworld.org

Gray Ghost Ventures: Impact investment firm dedicated to providing market-based capital solutions to entrepreneurs who are addressing the needs of low-income communities.
http://www.grayghostventures.com

Kopernik: Connecting tools and people where it is most needed.
http://thekopernik.org/

MicroPlace: Enables investors to fund microfinance projects.
https://www.microplace.com

Project H Design: Brings design to the socially overlooked.
http://projecthdesign.org

SA Social Investment Exchange (SASIX): Social investment stock exchange where select projects are listed and offered to the public as investment opportunities with a social return.
http://www.sasix.co.za

Ushahidi: Aggregates information from the public for use in crisis response.
http://ushahidi.com

KIDS' STUFF

No matter how badly you want your little girl to fit into that itty-bitty, polka-dot dress forever, she simply won't. Kids grow like weeds. But Mesh businesses have a solution to the headache of children's clothing: swapping. Exchange platforms enable families to swap everything from cloth diapers to maternity wear while saving money and limiting resource consumption at the same time. Mesh organizations also use information technology to connect families interested in sharing advice about parenting, cloth diapering, and more.

Looking to clean out your baby's closet or find great kids' stuff for free? Freepeats is a convenient way for parents to recycle baby, kid, and maternity items, including clothing, high chairs, swings, bikes, toys, and bouncers. As long as an item is safe, gently worn, and has no missing parts, Freepeats allows members to post an "offer" (a brief description of what they're giving away) on their Web site. Members are welcome to peruse offers in fifty-four cities and, upon finding something of interest, contact other members directly to arrange a pickup time and location. Freepeats offers free lifetime membership when you register during your city's free enrollment period.

Baby Swap: Maternity and used baby goods swap platform.
http://www.babyswap.net

Beers for Books: Beers for Books raises money for childhood literacy in developing countries.
http://www.beersforbooks.org

BoxKids: Brazilian-based company that allows families to swap children's clothes.
http://www.boxkids.com.br

Children's Music Foundation: The Children's Music Foundation supports and elevates academic achievement for elementary school children through music.
http://cmfinc.org

dimdom: Toy rental service in the U.K.
http://www.dimdom.fr

KidsKarton: Web site for online clothing swaps in Germany.
http://www.kidskarton.de

Quest to Learn: A school that supports the digital lives of children.
http://q2l.org

Savvy Auntie: Online community for aunts.
http://www.savvyauntie.com

StorkBrokers: An online marketplace that allows parents to sell their no longer needed baby and kid items.
http://www.storkbrokers.com

Swap Baby Goods: Baby goods swaps.
http://www.swapbabygoods.com

MAKING STUFF

In this category, Mesh companies help clients design and produce personalized products, such as custom-printed fabrics. They also create online marketplaces where crafters and DIY enthusiasts share their projects and sell handmade creations.

Build. Craft. Hack. Play. Make. Sound appealing? Check out Maker Faire, the two-day, family-friendly event series that celebrates creatives who like to tinker and love to make things. Maker Faire aims to inspire, unite, inform, and entertain a growing community of highly imaginative people who undertake jaw-dropping projects in their basements, backyards, and garages. At the event, Makers share their innovative DIY projects and skills. Maker Bob Schneeveis, for example, showcases his fantastical electric vehicles, including a redesigned Corbin Sparrow motorcycle. Maker Faire offers advanced tickets on its Web site.

bildr: Visual Web-based library of instruction sets.
http://bildr.org

Bon Bon Kakku: Custom fabric design site.
http://www.bonbonkakku.com

Craftster: Online community that shares hip DIY projects.
http://www.craftster.org/forum

Etsy: Handmade goods marketplace.
http://www.etsy.com

Fab Lab Bcn: Uses digital art to create objects.
http://www.fablabbcn.org

Fabric on Demand: Custom-printed fabrics.
http://www.fabricondemand.com

MyCraft: Social network for crafters.
http://www.mycraft.com

100kGarages: Community of workshops with digital fabrication tools.
http://www.100kgarages.com

Ponoko: Online marketplace for making real things.
http://www.ponoko.com

ThreadBanger: ThreadBanger is the home of DIY fashion
how-tos and home decor tips.
http://www.youtube.com/threadbanger

MARKETING SERVICES

Mesh companies pioneer Internet-enabled strategies to determine what products or services may be of interest to consumers,
build brand identity, and offer other unique, affordable marketing services. FreshlyBranded, for example, helps buyers advertise
their marketing needs on the Web and solicits designs and ideas
from creative professionals for the buyer to purchase. Other
Meshy organizations use advanced data capacity for tracking and
aggregating customer information to help businesses engage
and expand their target markets.

Are you a trendsetter who loves to shout about the things you love?
Hollrr hopes so. It's a new platform that makes it easy to share
recommendations for great new products. Driven by the desire to
help underdog companies launch new products, Hollrr encourages businesses to list their products on the Web site so fans can
demonstrate their support. As on Twitter, Hollrr users can follow
other people to keep track of the cool products they discover
and recommend. Users also earn points and unlock badges for
making great recommendations. Nothing is more valuable than
a positive word-of-mouth recommendation.

AcademixDirect: Education marketing. Connects students
to their ideal universities.
http://www.academixdirect.com

Carrotmob: Carrotmob harnesses consumer power to make it possible for the most socially responsible business practices to also be the most profitable choices.
http://carrotmob.org

Earthsite: Marketing and strategy for sustainable brands.
http://www.earthsite.net

Green Octopus Consulting: Green Octopus Consulting is a sustainability strategy and communications firm that helps create and promote vibrant, livable communities.
http://www.greenoctopus.net

LeadVine: Online social community that connects companies with new customers.
http://www.leadvine.com

Mozes: Helps music and event marketers use mobile services to build audiences.
http://www.mozes.com

Scout Labs: Collaborative platform for companies and their agents to listen to customers and engage them online.
http://www.scoutlabs.com

Sharethrough: Sharethrough works with the world's top brands and media companies to distribute their brand videos online and to track and maximize views and engagement.
http://www.sharethrough.com

Skibsted Ideation A/S: Uses design as a marketing tool.
http://www.skibstedid.com

MISCELLANEOUS

Thousands of Mesh businesses are thriving, from small start-ups to large cap companies. Among the more difficult to categorize include businesses that offer dog rentals, crowdsource creative ideas, run design contests, and aim to conserve resources by connecting couriers with people who want to send parcels. In this category, you will find a whole host of miscellaneous Mesh businesses.

In his third year at UCLA, Chuck Gordon needed to move out of his Los Angeles apartment before spending a semester abroad in Singapore. Faced with exorbitant storage costs, Gordon was forced to get creative. Enter his idea for SpareFoot, an online marketplace for self-storage listings in the United States. The process is easy: individuals with space to rent (including spare closets, garages, or extra bedrooms) post a listing on SpareFoot and wait for a renter to be in touch. Now, less than two years since its launch, SpareFoot has the largest inventory of storage options on the Web. Renters can choose from upward of 100,000 listings, which include space made available by both private renters and self-storage companies.

Colis-Voiturage: Connects package senders with couriers.
http://www.colis-voiturage.com

Crowdcast: Provider of collective intelligence solutions that help companies make better-informed decisions.
http://crowdcast.com

Flexpetz: Dogs and other pets on "loan."
http://www.flexpetz.com

Futerra Sustainability Communications: Communications agency focused on strategies for marketing corporate responsibility and sustainability.
http://www.futerra.co.uk

NineSigma: Open innovation service provider.
http://www.ninesigma.com

99designs: Helps companies run a design contest in which designers compete to create a design to meet their needs.
http://99designs.com

PledgeBank: Helps people use a pledge system to get things done.
http://www.pledgebank.com

SpareFoot: Storage listings for locations including your local self-storage facility and your neighbor's garage.
http://www.sparefoot.com

Spareground: Advertise or search for accommodation, storage, land, parking, and more.
http://www.spareground.co.uk

TheyWorkForYou: Resource for citizens to keep tabs on the U.K.'s parliaments and assemblies.
http://www.theyworkforyou.com

MUSIC AND FILM

Mesh businesses leverage the power of the Web to connect communities of music and film enthusiasts who collaborate, share expertise, form bands, and discover new artists and films. Some companies make specific offers to musicians, including guitar rentals, marketing advice, and booking services. Other Mesh businesses use online platforms to offer music recommendations and DVD rentals.

Do you think the radio sounds like a broken record? With declining music sales, record labels have begun to sign fewer artists, which makes it nearly impossible for new talent to make it big. That is, until now. The creators of SellaBand have designed an alternative funding model in hopes of turning the music industry on its ear. Their grand idea: a "fan funding model." Through SellaBand, artists can raise money from their fans to record professional albums. "Believers," or music fans interested in supporting SellaBand artists, buy "Parts" of an artist, which means that they donate money that will be held in escrow until the artist achieves her fund-raising goal. At all times before the artist reaches her target, Believers have the option to withdraw their money and move it to another project. At minimum, Believers get to download an album for free, but they may earn other rewards (such as autographed T-shirts, lifetime backstage passes, or even autographed instruments) for their contributions.

Bandmix: Brings musicians and bands together.
http://www.bandmix.com

Bandstocks: Collaboration platform for music fans and artists.
http://www.bandstocks.com

Creative Commons: Provides a standardized way to grant copyright permissions to creative work.
http://creativecommons.org

GigMaven: Free online gig booking for musicians.
http://gigmaven.com

Guitar Affair: Offers guitar rentals.
http://www.guitaraffair.com

MuckWork: Helps musicians manage the business of being a musician.
http://www.muckwork.com

OB Cooperative Records: Cooperative record label.
http://obcooperativerecords.com

Seventymm: Movie rental service in India.
http://www.seventymm.com

Songkick: Songkick is an online database of concerts for music enthusiasts that lets you track the music you like, create a personalized concert calendar, and buy tickets.
http://www.songkick.com

SoundCloud: SoundCloud is a platform that puts your sound at the heart of communities, Web sites, and even apps.
http://soundcloud.com

Tribe of Noise: Music community that connects artists, fans, and professionals.
http://www.tribeofnoise.com

NATURAL RESOURCE MANAGEMENT

Natural resource management organizations aim to protect the health and diversity of biological systems by designing sustainable initiatives. In this category you will find Mesh companies that use sophisticated technology to create and implement rainwater collection devices, forest restoration strategies, graywater recycling systems, ecosystem financial products, and other environment-centered projects.

Today, flush toilets account for 30 percent of the freshwater consumption in the average American home. Taken in consideration with a recent projection that at least thirty-six states will face water shortages by the year 2012, Water Legacy believes we cannot afford for this consumption rate to continue. The company has designed a graywater system that recycles domestic bathing water for use in flush toilets. It's simple. The system collects used water from baths and showers, filters and disinfects it, and then supplies the graywater to toilets on demand. Households that adopt the new technology, says Water Legacy, will reduce their domestic freshwater consumption by 30 percent.

Carbon Disclosure Project: The Carbon Disclosure Project is an independent not-for-profit organization holding the largest database of primary corporate climate change information in the world.
https://www.cdproject.net

EKO Asset Management Partners: Investment firm focused on building partnerships that monetize unrealized services provided by natural systems.
http://www.ekoamp.com

Environmental Entrepreneurs: Community of business leaders who advocate for strong environmental policies.
http://www.e2.org

Environmental Expert: Connects environmental experts and provides resources including marketing services, publications, job postings, and more.
http://www.environmental-expert.com

Nursery Technology Cooperative: Restoration technology for the Pacific Northwest's forests.
http://ferm.forestry.oregonstate.edu

Rainwater HOG: The Rainwater HOG is a modular rainwater and emergency water storage system.
http://rainwaterhog.com

Water Legacy: Designs graywater recycling systems.
http://www.waterlegacy.com

REAL ESTATE

The list of shareable goods and services in the Mesh is virtually unlimited. For individuals who are willing to live or work together, even space itself becomes a shareable physical resource. For example, coworking spaces provide freelancers access to stimulating, hot-desk environments where people work side by side, collaborate, and share best practices. Shared living arrangements and apartment sublets also fall into this category. Mesh organizations commonly use Internet-enabled platforms to connect renters with property owners in an effort to make the renting process more efficient.

As people begin to reconsider what's valuable and important, many see the need for new models that blend social and environmental values with economic viability—the need to work together in high-performing systems. But where might this collaboration take place? At the Hub. It's a coworking space, event series, and professional toolset for a community of more than 5,000 social and environmental change agents. Hub spaces connect members to increase idea flow and collaboration through peer-to-peer mentoring, professional consulting, and brown bag dialogues. The Hub offers five levels of membership, priced according to designated hours of desk time. Through membership, changemakers also gain access to more than twenty global Hub locations and the ability to connect virtually through Hub+, an online social networking platform.

AltSpace: AltSpace is a dedicated, cost effective, coworking space in Wellington, NZ.
http://www.altspace.co.nz

Citizen Space: Coworking space located in San Francisco, California.
http://citizenspace.us

FROGBOX: FROGBOX offers a convenient, affordable, and eco-friendly alternative to cardboard moving boxes.
http://frogbox.com

In Good Company: Shared workspace for female business owners.
http://www.ingoodcompanyworkplaces.com

Instant: Matches businesses with available office space.
http://www.instantoffices.com

Loosecubes: Loosecubes helps you find a shared office space where you can work.
http://loosecubes.com

Roomster: Online community for roommate shares, apartments, and sublets.
http://www.roomster.com

SuiteMatch: Web site for finding and posting shared office space.
http://suitematch.com

thinkspace: Provides shared coworking space, virtual offices, and meeting rooms.
http://thinkspace.com

Workspring: Offers modern studio workspace for rent.
http://www.workspring.com

HOME EXCHANGE ORGANIZATIONS

Real estate exchange organizations arrange home swaps between members on both short-term and permanent bases. Signing up for a membership will allow you to list multiple properties, participate in home exchanges during prime-time weeks, link to a personal Web site from your listings, and gain access to a complete list of available properties. Some home exchange companies cater exclusively to specific demographics, such as teachers on sabbatical.

Vacation Rentals by Owner (VRBO) is an online platform where homeowners advertise vacation properties and travelers find affordable, private accommodations around the world. For just under $300 a year, you can join VRBO, create a profile, and list your properties. Over 85,000 individual property owners currently offer their homes through the online platform, giving travelers access to over 130,000 listings in one hundred countries. Travelers now choose from private rental properties and fine private homes, condos, and apartments offered through management companies and rental agencies. With VRBO, travelers get big savings on nightly rates, unbeatable privacy, and all the comforts of home.

Aussie House Swap: Online home exchange company.
http://www.aussiehouseswap.com.au

Best House Swap: Facilitates permanent real estate exchanges.
http://besthouseswap.com

Exchange deMaison: Facilitates international home exchange.
http://www.echangeimmo.com

Exclusive Resorts: Global luxury home and resort travel club.
http://www.exclusiveresorts.com

Pad4Pad: Real estate Web site where users find vacation swaps, houses for sale, and foreclosure listings.
http://www.pad4pad.com

Permanent House Trading: Facilitates permanent home exchange.
http://permanenthousetrading.com

ProfVac: Home exchange service for educators.
http://www.profvac.com

RoofSwap: Offers international home exchanges.
http://www.roofswap.com

Swaptogo: Home exchange service based in the U.K.
http://www.houseswaptogo.co.uk

3rd Home: Luxury home exchange program.
http://wadeshealy.3rdhome.com

Vacation Rentals by Owner (VRBO): Online space for homeowners to advertise their vacation properties.
http://www.vrbo.com

SKILLS

Using Internet-enabled share platforms, the Mesh makes it easy for people to connect with others and share expertise. Organizations will allow an individual to display her skills on the Web or find others who have the expertise she needs. Through share platforms, users can then build relationships, make agreements, and share or swap their skills. In this category you will also find Meshy companies that help small businesses get expert advice from creative professionals.

FriendlyFavor is an all-purpose request tool that enables you to easily ask, offer, and manage online favors. Whether you're looking for a ride to the airport, a recommendation for good eats, or a dog sitter, FriendlyFavor will help you reach out to your "peeps"— your trusted network of friends, family, and colleagues. And it's efficient. Instead of sorting through endless e-mail threads, FriendlyFavor sends an appeal to your peeps using your existing e-mail lists and then archives any responses (Think Evite). The Web site also helps you repay the favor with an exchange of services, gift certificates, or charitable donations.

Amazon Mechanical Turk: Marketplace for work.
https://www.mturk.com

crowdSPRING: Offers affordable graphic design and writing services to small businesses by connecting consumers with creative professionals.
http://www.crowdspring.com

fiverr: The place for people to share things they're willing to do for $5.
http://fiverr.com

Guru: Members find freelancers at Guru's online service marketplace.
http://www.guru.com

Ideas Culture: Offers a team of Idea Agents to help create a company's next big idea.
http://www.ideasculture.com

SkillPages: Helps you find skilled people and get noticed.
http://www.skillpages.com

Squidoo: Passionate experts share advice and direct
seekers to best resources.
www.squidoo.com

Swapaskill: Swap something you can do for what you need.
http://www.swapaskill.com

TaskRabbit: Service networking. Users network to get their
errands done.
http://taskrabbit.com

SOCIAL NETWORKING

The newest wave of information technology enables Mesh businesses to unite people with common interests through social networks. Members of these online platforms can engage in conversation, exchange information, share photos, and form special-interest groups. Other Mesh companies in this category use advanced data capacity for tracking and aggregating information to analyze and report trends that develop on social networking sites.

Do, learn, share, or change something. That's what you'll do as a member of Meetup, a network of local groups that meet up face-to-face. Driven by the goal to improve their community or themselves, more than 2,000 groups get together in their local communities every day. And with 68,000 local groups to choose from, you're likely to find a group that meets your needs, whether you want to learn how to pair wine and cheese, practice Arabic, or play flag football. But if you don't find an appealing Meetup group, you can start one yourself. The Web site will help you pick a theme, find members, make plans, and schedule your first Meetup.

Eat With Me: Eat With Me allows you to meet new people in your neighborhood by organizing and attending events and sharing a meal together.
http://eatwithme.net

Fotolog: Social networking site for photo bloggers.
http://www.fotolog.com

Green Drinks: Meetups for people in the environmental field.
http://www.greendrinks.org

Klout: Measures influence across the social Web and allows you to track the impact of your opinions, links, and recommendations.
http://klout.com

LinkedIn: Service for colleagues, former colleagues, and friends to network.
http://www.linkedin.com

Meetup: Network of local interest groups that meet face-to-face. Users organize groups or join them.
http://www.meetup.com

Please Rob Me: Raises awareness about the danger in over-sharing location-based information.
http://pleaserobme.com

Schoolwires: Provides online communication, Web site, and community management tools to schools.
http://www.schoolwires.com

Shareable: Online blog that tells the story of sharing.
http://shareable.net

Springspotters: Global online community that reports new business ideas.
http://www.springspotters.com

Twitturly: Ranks and tracks what URLs people are talking about on Twitter.
http://twitturly.com

TECHNOLOGY

Companies in this category use new technology to develop tools and platforms for enabling the Mesh. This includes sophisticated information systems, as mentioned previously, that track and aggregate consumer data to make sharing possible. Online photo-sharing sites, for example, use Mesh-friendly technology not only to help users upload, store, and share pictures with their social networks but also to make timely, customized offers (such as baby-themed photo albums) to consumers. Similarly, open-source share platforms use advanced data capacity to make valuable information available to the public. You'll find these models, and others, in this category.

In 2009 a new civic engagement tool called CitySourced hit the streets in San Jose, California, allowing citizens to identify and report civic issues on the go. Using the CitySourced smartphone application, people can file sightings of graffiti, littering, potholes, and so on to city hall. Think of it as civic crowdsourcing. The app lets you photograph an infraction and locate it via your phone's GPS tracking device. Once the image uploads successfully, users can then add comments about the problem and share it on Twitter as well. It's a techy occasion for government to improve citizen accountability.

Celltradeusa: Enables dissatisfied cell phone customers to get out of their service contracts by finding others who want in.
http://www.celltradeusa.com

Citizens Connect iPhone App: Aims to gather information about Boston, Massachusetts, from residents and visitors.
www.cityofboston.gov/mis/apps/iphone.asp

Drupal: Open-source content management platform.
http://drupal.org

esloúltimo: Enables communication between brands and consumers.
http://www.esloultimo.com

FleetCommander: Web-based fleet management system that can be used for car-sharing services.
http://www.agilefleet.com

Knotpic: The easiest way to collect all of your photos to make a brilliant gallery and slideshow of your big day.
http://knotpic.com

Open311: Provides open communication with public services and local government.
http://open311.org

SkiReport: iPhone application that gives users access to information about ski areas.
http://www.skireport.com/iphone

TechForward: Offers members a guaranteed buyback plan with their next computer or consumer electronic purchase.
http://www.techforward.com

The Extraordinaries: Smartphone application that enables people to complete micro-tasks for organizations, causes, or people.
http://www.beextra.org

YouNoodle: Users discover and support early-stage companies.
http://younoodle.com

TRANSPORTATION

Mesh companies make sharing cars and bikes more convenient and fun—and less expensive—than owning them, while increasing the efficiency of our transportation systems. As a member of a car-sharing company, you can reserve a vehicle on an hourly, daily, or weekly basis. A personal key (such as a Zipcard) gives you access to the car-sharing fleet so you can drive away in a clean, maintained, and fully insured vehicle anywhere, anytime. Another car-sharing model allows you to rent your personal vehicle to drivers in your neighborhood. Think of it as peer-to-peer car sharing. Companies that enable these car-sharing marketplaces help you set a rental price, schedule the hours your car will be available for use, connect with member drivers, and make extra money. Similarly, bike-sharing companies allow members to rent bicycles for any length of time. Other Meshy transportation companies help consumers trade cars and boats, share taxicabs, and gain access to information about public transportation.

Interested in starting your own car-sharing service? The Paris-based company Eileo will steer you down the right road. It offers customized tools—including GPS, RFID, full Web-based car-sharing software, and noninvasive hardware installation—to cover all your car-sharing technology needs, from registration to invoicing. Eileo's team of engineers is available 24/7 to help you continuously improve your car-sharing business. And their complete solutions will enable you to partner with other car-sharing services worldwide. When you expand your network to include partners in the same city or anywhere in the world, members will enjoy the same benefits of car sharing wherever they go.

Bicas: A community education and recycling center for bicycles that welcomes people of all ages and walks of life.
http://bicas.org

Bicing: Urban public transit by bicycle in Barcelona.
http://www.bicing.com

Eileo: Provides the necessary technology for starting a car-sharing service.
http://www.eileo.com

GoLoco: Ride-sharing system that notifies users when their friends or interest groups are going places they want to go.
http://www.goloco.org

Greenwheels: German car-sharing company.
http://www.greenwheels.de

GTFS Data Exchange: Provides open-source information about public transportation.
http://www.gtfs-data-exchange.com

liftshare: Ride-sharing service that connects passengers and drivers in the U.K.
http://www.liftshare.com/uk

MyTTC: Provides open access to transit data.
http://myttc.ca

NuRide: Users track their savings and earn rewards for carpooling, biking, walking, telecommuting, or using public transportation.
http://www.nuride.com

OYBike: Street-based rental station technology that allows users to hire and return a bicycle via their mobile phone.
http://www.oybike.com

SpotScout: Enables drivers to find parking via their desktop and mobile phone.
http://www.spotscout.com

Swapalease: Helps customers get out of a car lease by transferring the lease to a qualified buyer.
http://www.swapalease.com

TRAVEL

Mesh companies that offer travel-related goods and services are a great way for people to gain access to affordable accommodations; vibrant, travel-centered communities; and reliable travel advice. Mesh companies that offer home or room rentals, for instance, give globetrotters the opportunity to vacation on the cheap. Partnering with these companies is also an easy way for homeowners with spare rooms to earn cash and meet new people. Online social networks allow travel enthusiasts to form communities and exchange stories, tips, and photos from past trips. Other Mesh companies offer vacation-planning services.

Want to sleep on a futon in Tokyo, a couch in Seville, or a twin in California . . . for free? Driven by the goal of strengthening our global community, CouchSurfing aims to build meaningful connections across cultures by enabling residents worldwide to host a diverse group of travelers. The catch: you will likely find yourself sleeping on a living room couch. To get started, both travelers and hosts set up profiles, define their expectations, and start connecting. The best way to verify a CouchSurfer is to check out his or her references, the required evaluations written by both surfers and hosts at the end of a stay.

Airbnb: Online marketplace allowing anyone, from private residents to commercial property managers, to rent out their extra space.
http://www.airbnb.com

CouchSurfing: Connects travelers with locals. Enables members to share hospitality.
http://www.couchsurfing.org

Dopplr: Members share personal and business travel plans with their private networks.
http://www.dopplr.com

Driftr: Platform for sharing travel information.
http://www.driftr.com

EveryTrail: Platform for geo-tagged, user-generated travel content.
http://www.everytrail.com

Planely: Planely is a "social flying revolution" that allows you to meet some new people who enjoy flying.
http://www.planely.com

SabbaticalHomes: Internet-based directory for academic home exchanges, home rentals, and house-sitting opportunities.
http://sabbaticalhomes.com

SingleSpotCamping: Connects landowners with camping guests.
http://www.singlespotcamping.com

TravellingTogether.EU: Connects people who want travel partners.
http://www.travellingtogether.eu

waze: Crowdsourced maps in real time.
www.waze.com

UPCYCLING, RECYCLING, AND WASTE MANAGEMENT

Mesh organizations aim to extend the useful life of products and reduce waste in landfills by facilitating material exchanges among individuals and businesses. They also decrease raw material resource demand by offering creative recycling services, including airport trolley upcycling, electronic and commercial waste recycling, and more.

Reduce, reuse, recycle: The concept has been around for years, but new incentives for recycling are anything but old school. Take RecycleBank. It's a rewards and loyalty program that issues

RecycleBank points to reward households for their recycling efforts. The company helps municipalities and haulers track the amount of recyclables collected each week, and then rewards points to households based on the weight of their recycled materials. RecycleBank points can be redeemed at over 1,500 local and national businesses that support recycling, including Kashi Company, Ikea, Coca-Cola Company, Nature Made, and Home Depot. Today, RecycleBank serves over one million people in twenty states across the United States. That number will likely explode when RecycleBank goes global: the service plans to launch in Europe this summer.

A Box Life: Keeps shippable cardboard boxes in use longer.
http://www.aboxlife.com

AuH2O: Sells clothing made of recycled materials.
http://www.auh2odesigns.com

bordbar: Upcycles airport luggage trolleys.
http://www.bordbar.de

Cottong. From Blue to Green: Upcycles denim garments into natural cotton fiber insulation.
http://www.cottonfrombluetogreen.org

ecofindeRRR: iPhone application that lets you discover where to recycle and dispose of waste products.
http://www.ecofinderapp.com

Empties4Cash: Recycling program that offers fund-raising opportunities.
http://www.empties4cash.com

Gigoit: A site that enables communities to exchange reusable items.
http://www.gigoit.org

NextWorth: Evaluates used electronic devices and exchanges them for a check, gift card, or e-gift.
http://www.nextworth.com

2Good2Toss: Online exchange platform for reusable building materials and household items.
http://www.2good2toss.com

Unpackaged: Bulk food store that requires consumers to bring their own containers or use reusable bags.
http://beunpackaged.com

YouRenew: Recycling service for electronic devices.
http://www.yourenew.com

Acknowledgments

I have always known that the people who surround me, who share themselves and their inspirations, concerns, and fears in genuine ways are truly treasures. The creation of this book has called on me in entirely new ways than any other project I've undertaken previously, and no one has been more unstoppably generous, wise, honest, and wonderfully present than my dear friend Seth Godin. You are a dear, brilliant, bald, and spectacular gift. Thank you in all ways, always.

This being my first book (yes, presumptuous), I was again graced with a talented team of characters to flesh out, refine, develop, and design all things Mesh related. Led by the talented, well humored, and pathologically soft-spoken Kerry Tremain, what many people warned me would be a horrific experience was entirely divine.

Kerry, your focus, pace, and understated magnetism helped to make this book something I am, and I hope you and the team are, very proud of. Thanks to Jessica Conrad, whose intensity, talents, and long hours did not go unnoticed; and to Joe Loya for his undying humor, sharp eye, and well-timed interruptions. To Eric Irvine who picked up the slack, stepping in without needing to be asked. To Julia Flagg Leaver, a great designer who has been two steps ahead, quietly anticipating and ridiculously low maintenance, a gem. And to Surendra and the team who seem to consistently manage to pull rabbits out of hidden hats. Thank you.

In the days of The Mesh "on simmer," before I could fully embrace and envision this book as a project, Joaquina Peña, Saul Griffith, Andrew Blau, Steven Addis, Stuart and Karen Gansky, Megan Casey, and Bob Morgan fed the flame, made harsh facial expressions, and shared liberally. I so appreciate your time, candor, curiosity, friendship, and openness.

Luis Sota, Todd Lash, Peter Schwartz, Eamonn Kelly, Maria Guidice, Nancy Murphy, Chris Anderson, Sunny Bates, Christie Dames, Kevin O'Malley, Juan Enriquez, Jacqueline Novogratz, Ethan Beard, Joel Makower, Laurie Coots, Shawn Gensch, Mitchell Baker, Chris Beard, John Lilly, Joi Ito, Denise Caruso, and Lisa Minucci all contributed to my thinking, reshaping, and concern for sharing The Mesh effectively and well. Thank you for your time, insights, and support.

To my team at Portfolio, you are, as A.Z. would say, "the bomb"! Thanks for the dedication, alacrity, vision, tenacity, and partnership. Special thanks to those I perhaps wore out the most: Will Weisser, Joe Perez, Rachel Burd, Miranda Ottewell, Alissa Amell, Pauline Neuwirth, Lance Fitzgerald, Maureen Cole, and my unflappable, resilient, and talented editor, Courtney Young, and to the chief "bomb," Adrian Zackheim, who I am thrilled to have as my publisher. You have made this whole experience something I am eager to repeat. Thank you for your generosity and trust.

For my agent, Lisa DiMona, who saw The Mesh as I was learning to speak its language. She has been a faithful and exuberant colleague, fan, and friend.

Some people have a kind of "impact echo." While we may not have been wildly discussing this book per se, Tim O'Reilly, Dale Dougherty, Bill McDonough, Bob Epstein, Larry Lessig, Esther Dyson, Jane Goodall, and Paul Hawken have left me frequently provoked, and for that I thank you.

The Mesh References

Adams, Anna. "Sharing Gardens to Grow Veg." *BBC News*, February 26, 2009, http://news.bbc.co.uk/2/hi/uk_news/7911975.stm (accessed March 17, 2010).

Adejobi, Alicia. "Credit Crunch Forces Smart Shopping: UK Boutiques and Clothes Swapping Parties." *Orato*, August 18, 2009, http://www.orato.com/home-family/credit-crunch-forces-smart-shopping (accessed March 16, 2010).

Alexander, Christopher. *The Timeless Way of Building*. New York: Oxford University Press, 1979.

Alter, Lloyd. "9 Hip Housing Alternatives to the Mortgaged Single Family Home." *Planet Green*, November 3, 2009, http://planetgreen.discovery.com/home-garden/hip-housing-alternatives.html (accessed March 17, 2010).

Anderson, Chris. *The Long Tail: Why the Future of Business Is Selling Less of More*. New York: Hyperion, 2006.

Belson, Ken. "Car-Sharing Services Cut Cost of Ownership." *New York Times*, October 20, 2009, http://www.nytimes.com/2009/10/22/automobiles/autospecial2/22ZIP.html (accessed March 17, 2010).

Bernoff, Josh, and Charlene Li. *Groundswell: Winning in a World Transformed by Social Technologies*. Boston: Forrester Research, 2008.

Brand, Stewart. *How Buildings Learn: What Happens after They're Built.* New York: Penguin Press, 1995.

Braungart, Michael, and William McDonough. *Cradle to Cradle: Remaking the Way We Make Things.* New York: North Point Press, 2002.

Brown, Tim. *Change by Design: How Design Thinking Transforms Organizations and Inspires Innovation.* New York: Harper Business, 2009.

Burt, Ronald S. *Neighbor Networks: Competitive Advantage Local and Personal.* New York: Oxford University Press, 2009.

Bush, Mark. "Matching House Sitters with House Owners: One Company's Matchmaking Service." PowerHomeBiz.com, http://www.powerhomebiz.com/News/092009/match-home-sitters.htm (accessed March 17, 2010).

Cafferky, Monica. "Swap Until You Drop!" Mirror.co.uk, March 2, 2010, http://www.mirror.co.uk/news/top-stories/2010/02/03/swap-until-you-drop-115875-22014971 (accessed March 16, 2010).

Carew, Emma L. "Hotels Too Pricey? Try a Swap." *Washington Post,* September 26, 2009, http://www.washingtonpost.com/wp-dyn/content/article/2009/09/24/AR2009092405338.html (accessed March 17, 2010).

Chase, Allan. "Sun Ra: Musical Change and Musical Meaning in the Life and Work of a Jazz Composer." M.A. thesis, Tufts University, 1992.

Cheeseman, Gina-Marie. "Best Buy's Environmental Efforts." TriplePundit, October 12, 2009, http://www.triplepundit.com/2009/10/best-buys-environmental-efforts (accessed March 25, 2010).

Christakis, Nicholas A., and James H. Fowler. *Connected: The Surprising Power of Our Social Networks and How They Shape Our Lives.* New York: Little, Brown and Company, 2009.

Christian, Sena. "The Growth of Citizen Co-Ops Is a Positive Development As Corporations Fail Us in Every Way." *AlterNet,*

January 5, 2010, http://www.alternet.org/workplace/144969/ business_as_usual_is_history:_corporations_won%27t_save _us,_but_co-ops_may (accessed March 16, 2010).

Cornell, Lauren. "Rhizome.org: Enhancing Artistic Collaboration Online." iFOCOS, February 5, 2007, http://ifocos.org/2007/ 02/05/rhizomeorg-enhancing-artistic-collaboration-online (accessed March 16, 2010).

Cosenza, Vincenzo. "World Map of Social Networks." *Vincos Blog*, http://www.vincos.it/world-map-of-social-networks (accessed March 18, 2010).

Crawford, Joel. "Carfree Conversations: Making Today's Cities Carfree." *Carbusters*, March 1, 2010, http://carbusters .org/2009/11/18/making-today%E2%80%99s-cities-carfree (accessed March 17, 2010).

Crider, Caleb. "The Low Tech Movement." *Examiner.com*, September 1, 2009, http://www.examiner.com/x-20733-Portland-Emerging-Church-Examiner~y2009m9d1-The-low-tech-movement (accessed March 17, 2010).

Crislip, Kathleen. "Couchsurfing—Cross Cultural Lodging Concept." *About.com*, http://studenttravel.about.com/od/ lodgingwithatwist/p/couchsurfing.htm (accessed March 17, 2010).

Das, Anupreeta. "LG, Netflix to Launch TVs with Instant Movie Viewing." *USA Today*, January 5, 2009, http://www .usatoday.com/tech/products/gear/2009-01-05-lg-netflix _N.htm (accessed March 24, 2010).

Diller, Steve, Darrel Rhea, and Nathan Shedroff. *Making Meaning: How Successful Businesses Deliver Meaningful Customer Experiences.* Berkeley, Calif.: New Riders, 2006.

Doskow, Emily, and Janelle Orsi. *The Sharing Solution: How to Save Money, Simplify Your Life & Build Community.* Berkeley, Calif.: Nolo, 2009.

Fausset, Katherine, Sharon Cohen Fredman, Rebecca Sample Gerstung, Cynthia Harris, Lucia Quartararo, and Lisa Singer. *The Cooking Club Cookbook: Six Friends Show You How to Bake, Broil, and Bond.* New York: Villard Books, 2002.

Feld, Brad. "The Ultimate Travel Community Site." *FeldThoughts*, April 26, 2007, http://www.feld.com/wp/archives/2007/04/the-ultimate-travel-community-site.html (accessed March 18, 2010).

Fleischer, Deborah. "Employee Engagement: AngelPoints and Saatchi S Launch New PSP Tool." *TriplePundit*, October 27, 2009, http://www.triplepundit.com/2009/10/employee-engagement-angelpoints-and-saatchi-and-saatchi-s-launch-new-psp-tool (accessed March 17, 2010).

Flores, Heather Coburn. "How to Organize a Community Seed Swap." *Food Not Lawns International*, December 23, 2008, http://www.foodnotlawns.net/2008/12/how-to-organize-community-seed-swap_23.html.

Franson, Paul. "Microcrush Companies Cater to Niche Brands." *Wine Business Monthly*, August 15, 2006, http://www.winebusiness.com/wbm/?go=getArticle&dataId=44327 (accessed March 17, 2010).

Freedland, Jonathan. "Don't Just Howl with Rage: Try an Idea That Does Away with Banks Altogether." *Guardian*, August 18, 2009, http://www.guardian.co.uk/commentisfree/2009/aug/18/bankers-bonuses-credit-zopa (accessed March 17, 2010).

Garigliano, Jeff. "Swap Nation: Why Bartering Is Making a Comeback." *Reader's Digest.* http://www.rd.com/advice-and-know-how/swap-nation-why-bartering-is-making-a-comeback/article158312.html (accessed March 17, 2010).

Gawande, Atul. "Testing, Testing." *New Yorker*, December 14, 2009, http://www.newyorker.com/reporting/2009/12/14/091214fa_fact_gawande (accessed March 17, 2010).

Gilbert, Sarah. "Recession Tales: Bartering Exchanges 'Lame' for 'Hip'." *WalletPop*, November 11, 2005, http://www.walletpop .com/blog/2009/11/05/recession-tales-bartering-exchanges-lame-for-hip (accessed March 17, 2010).

Gipe, Paul. "Community-Owned Wind Development in Germany, Denmark, and the Netherlands." *Wind-Works.org*, 1996, http://www.wind-works.org/articles/Euro96TripReport .html (accessed March 17, 2010).

Godin, Seth. *Tribes: We Need You to Lead Us*. New York: Penguin Group, 2008.

GOOD: Bike Sharing. Video, 2009. YouTube, http://www.youtube .com/watch?v=jIFeSHCviuU (accessed March 18, 2010).

"Governors' Wind Energy Coalition Calls for National Renewable Energy Standard." *SustainableBusiness.com*, March 17, 2010, http://www.sustainablebusiness.com/index.cfm/go/news .display/id/19952 (accessed March 17, 2010).

Graham, Jefferson. "An iPhone Gets Zipcar Drivers on Their Way." *USA Today*, September 29, 2009, http://www.usatoday .com/tech/ products/2009-09-29-unlock-iphone-zipcar-tech_N.htm (accessed March 17, 2010).

Grant, John. *Co-opportunity: Join Up for a Sustainable, Resilient, Prosperous World*. Padstow, Cornwall, England: TJ International, 2010.

Hainer, Michelle. "Start Your Holiday Shopping Swapping." *Tonic*, November 10, 2009, http://www.tonic.com/article/holiday-home-accessories-swap (accessed March 17, 2010).

Harrison, John. "Bartering Taking Hold in Tough Times." *Business Journal*, July 3, 2009, http://www.bizjournals.com/ triad/stories/2009/07/06/story14.html (accessed March 17, 2010).

Hart, Sara. "A Platinum Setting: This 15-Acre, Mixed-Use, Harbor-Front Development in Victoria, B.C., Will Set Records for Sustainability at the Neighborhood Scale." *GreenSource*, January

2009, http://greensource.construction.com/projects/2009/01_DocksideGreen.asp (accessed March 17, 2010).

Helft, Miguel. "Rosensweig Lands at Textbook Renter Chegg .com." New York Times, February 3, 2010, http://dealbook.blogs .nytimes.com/2010/02/03/rosensweig-lands-at-textbook-renter-cheggcom/?partner=yahoofinance (accessed March 16, 2010).

Herbst, Kris. "Enabling the Poor to Build Housing: Cemex Combines Profit & Social Development." Changemakers, http://proxied.changemakers.net/journal/02september/herbst.cfm (accessed March 17, 2010).

Hill, Graham. "Tech-Enabled Bike Sharing Rolls into North America." Huffington Post, November 11, 2008, http://www .huffingtonpost.com/graham-hill/tech-enabled-bike-sharing_b_142885.html (accessed March 17, 2010).

"Home Exchange: Holidays/Vacations, Permanent, Council/Private Homes, New Build for Old, Crafts." Travel the Home Exchange Way, April 28, 2008, http://homeexchangetravel.blogs .com/home_exchange_travel/2008/04/home-exchange-h .html (accessed March 17, 2010).

Horchow, Sally. "Los Angeles Club Scene: Cooking Clubs." Food & Wine, November 2005, http://www.foodandwine.com/articles/los-angeles-club-scene-cooking-clubs (accessed March 17, 2010).

Hunt, Tara. The Whuffie Factor: Using the Power of Social Networks to Build Your Business. New York: Crown Business, 2009.

Jackson, Susan. "Swap Your Baby Stuff Online." Our365, http://www.our365.com/Wisdom/Moms/Swap%20Sites .aspx (accessed March 17, 2010).

James. "Keeping Track of Life." Nokia Conversations, August 26, 2008, http://conversations.nokia.com/2008/08/26/keeping-track-of-life (accessed March 18, 2010).

James, Denise. "Borrow Tools from a Local Library." *Action News*, August 23, 2009, http://abclocal.go.com/wpvi/story?section=news/local&id=6978571 (accessed March 17, 2010).

Jowit, Juliette. "Time to Clean Up: UN Study Reveals Environmental Cost of World Trads." *Guardian*, February 19, 2010, http://www.guardian.co.uk/environment/2010/feb/19/business-environmental-damage (accessed March 17, 2010).

Judkis, Maura. "Sharing Is Green (and Good for Your Wallet)." U.S. News & World Report, November 10, 2009, http://www.usnews.com/money/blogs/fresh-greens/2009/11/10/sharing-is-green-and-good-for-your-wallet.html (accessed March 17, 2010).

Kanter, Rosabeth Moss, and Stanley S. Litow. "Informed and Interconnected: A Manifesto for Smarter Cities." *Working Knowledge*, July 23, 2009, http://hbswk.hbs.edu/item/6238.html (accessed March 17, 2010).

Karp, Josh. "Building a Nation of Tinkerers: Digital Media Fosters Hands-On Learning in Science Labs." *Spotlight on Digital Media and Learning*, January 11, 2010, http://spotlight.macfound.org/btr/entry/building_nation_tinkerers_digital_media_hands-on_learning_science_labs (accessed March 16, 2010).

Kawasaki, Guy, and Matthew E. May. *In Pursuit of Elegance: Why the Best Ideas Have Something Missing*. New York: Random House, 2009.

Kilian, Jennifer, and Barbara Pantuso. "The Future of Health Care Is Social." *Fast Company*, October 6, 2009, http://www.fastcompany.com/future-of-health-care (accessed March 17, 2010).

Klein, Laura. "Organic Farming and the Future of Food." *TriplePundit*, October 29, 2009, http://www.triplepundit.com/2009/10/organic-farming-and-the-future-of-food (accessed March 17, 2010).

Korn, Melissa. "A Last-Minute Dash for Tuition." *Wall Street Journal*, August 19, 2009, http://online.wsj.com/article/SB10001424052 970203674704574336420044733980.html (accessed March 16, 2010).

Kristof, Nicholas D. "What Could You Live Without?" *New York Times*, January 23, 2010, http://www.nytimes .com/2010/01/24/opinion/24kristof.html (accessed March 17, 2010).

Learn, Scott. "Portland Ratchets Up Volunteer-Led 'Tool Libraries' That Lend Tools for Free." *Oregon Live*, January 8, 2010, http:// www.oregonlive.com/environment/index .ssf/2010/01/portland_ratchets_up_volunteer.html (accessed March 17, 2010).

LeCompte, Celeste. "Startups That Are Reinventing Carpooling on the Web." *GigaOM Network*, September 11, 2008, http://gigaom .com/2008/09/11/web-based-carpooling-startups-woo-the- enterprise-market (accessed March 17, 2010).

Lefteri, Chris. *Materials for Inspirational Design*. Singapore: RotoVision, 2006.

Lerman, Liz. "A Proposed Job Swap to Save American Capitalism." *Community Arts Network*, March 2009, http://www.community arts.net/readingroom/archivefiles/2009/03/a_proposed_job .php (accessed March 16, 2010).

Lew, Nate. "Colorado Electric Coop Offers Unique Solar Leasing Program." *CoolerPlanet*, September 15, 2009, http://www.solar .coolerplanet.com/News/9150902-colorado-electric-coop- offers-unique-solar-leasing-program.aspx (accessed March 17, 2010).

Lorica, Ben. "Google's New Marketplace Has Over a Thousand Apps." *O'Reilly Radar*, March 2010, http://radar.oreilly .com/2010/03/google-marketplace-has-over-a-thousand-apps .html (accessed March 18, 2010).

Lovins, Amory, L. Hunter Lovins, and Paul Hawken. *Natural Capitalism: Creating the Next Industrial Revolution*. Boston: Little, Brown and Company, 1999.

"Maker Faire Austin: Swap-O-Rama's Artist Open Call." *Make*, September 2007, http://blog.makezine.com/archive/2007/09/ maker_faire_austin_swapor.html (accessed March 16, 2010).

Martin, Jonathan. "Home Sweet Swap: House Exchange Opens Door to Adventure and Cultural Immersion." *Seattle Times*, September 27, 2009, http://seattletimes.nwsource.com/html/travel/2009936229_trhouseswap27.html (accessed March 17, 2010).

Martin, Justin. "Make Purchases without Cash." *Cable News Network*, June 23, 2009, http://money.cnn.com/2009/06/23/smallbusiness/fair_trade.fsb (accessed March 17, 2010).

Maxwell, Leanne. "This Weekend: Thread Fashion Event at Fort Mason." *sfist*, November 19, 2009, http://sfist.com/2009/11/19/this_weekend_thread_at_fort_mason_c.php (accessed March 16, 2010).

McCarthy, Bonnie. "Like Netflix for Your Closet: New Way to Swap Old Clothes." *WalletPop*, November 6, 2009, http://www.walletpop.com/blog/2009/11/06/like-netflix-for-your-closet-new-way-to-swap-old-clothes (accessed March 16, 2010).

Miemis, Venessa. "An Idea Worth Spreading: The Future Is Networks." *Emergent by Design*, March 16, 2010, http://emergentbydesign.com/2010/03/16/an-idea-worth-spreading-the-future-is-networks (accessed March 18, 2010).

Moodie, Clemmie. "Rent a Designer Handbag for as Little as £12.50 a Month." *Mail Online*, October 4, 2007, http://www.dailymail.co.uk/news/article-485503/Rent-designer-handbag-little-12-50-month.html (accessed March 16, 2010).

Morris, Alison. "A Photo Tour of the Montague Bookmill." *Publishers Weekly*, October 4, 2007, http://blogs.publishersweekly.com/blogs/shelftalker/?p=230 (accessed March 25, 2010).

Moss, Whitney. "How to Host a Clothing Swap." *Alphamom*, May 20, 2009, http://alphamom.com/family-fun/food-home/how-to-host-a-clothing-swap (accessed March 16, 2010).

Moya, Jared. "Grooveshark Offers Local Music Artists a Global Audience." *ZeroPaid*, August 16, 2007, http://www.zeropaid.com/news/8962/grooveshark_offers_local_music_artists_a_global_audience (accessed March 17, 2010).

Nakajima, Seio. "Film Clubs in Urban China: The Field of Cultural Consumption of Independent Films." *All Academic*, http://www.allacademic.com/meta/p_mla_apa_research_citation/1/8/2/6/2/p182621_index.html (accessed March 17, 2010).

"Naked Lady Party." *getcrafty*, http://www.getcrafty.com/home_nakedlady.php (accessed March 16, 2010).

"New Research by Millward Brown Reveals Amazon Is the Most Trusted and Recommended Brand in the U.S." *Millward Brown*, February 22, 2010, http://www.millwardbrown.com/global/news/pressreleases/PressReleaseDetails/10-02-22/New_Research_by_Millward_Brown_Reveals_Amazon_is_the_Most_Trusted_and_Recommended_Brand_in_the_U_S.aspx (accessed March 17, 2010).

O'Toole, Randal. "Population Growth and Cities." *Electronic Journal of Sustainable Development* 1, no. 3. (2009), http://www.ejsd.org/public/journal_article/15 (accessed March 18, 2010).

Owen, David. Green Metropolis: Why Living Smaller, Living Closer, and Driving Less Are the Keys to Sustainability. New York: Riverhead Books, 2009.

Padovani, Gigi, and Carlo Petrini. *Slow Food Revolution: A New Culture for Eating and Living*. New York: Columbia University Press, 2004.

Paquet, Laura. "Home Exchange—Stay in Europe for Free!" *Slow Europe*, August 2009 (updated May 2010), http://www.sloweurope.com/travel/plan/home-exchange.php (accessed March 17, 2010).

Paxton, Melissa. "Baja Fishermen Take Action to Save Endangered Sea Turtles." *Baja Life Online*, http://www.bajalife.com/ecowatch/seaturtles.html (accessed March 17, 2010).

"Peer-to-Peer Lending: How to Diversify Your Investment Portfolio with Peer-to-Peer Loans." *American Banking & Market News*, September 14, 2009, http://www.americanbankingnews.com/2009/09/14/how-to-diversify-your-investment-portfolio-with-peer-to-peer-loans (accessed March 17, 2010).

Poggi, Jeanine. "Blockbuster CEO: We Must 'Adapt or Die.'" *TheStreet*, February 5, 2010, http://www.thestreet.com/_yahoo/story/10674351/1/blockbuster-ceo-we-must-adapt-or-die.html (accessed March 17, 2010).

Pope, Justin. "College Textbooks Now for Rent." *SFGate*, August 14, 2009, http://www.sfgate.com/cgi-bin/article.cgi?f=/c/a/2009/08/14/BUQA198C6L.DTL (accessed March 16, 2010).

Price, Andrew. "Not a New York Minute." *Good*, January 11, 2010, http://www.good.is/post/not-a-new-york-minute (accessed March 17, 2010).

Randall, David K. "An Alternative to Student Loans? Peer-to-Peer Lending Sites Offer New Ways to Borrow Money." *Forbes.com*, August 26, 2009, http://www.forbes.com/2009/08/24/college-loans-alternative-personal-finance-peer-to-peer.html (accessed March 16, 2010).

Reece, Myers. "Flathead Electric Cooperative at Forefront of Renewable Energy." *Flathead Beacon*, August 26, 2009, http://www.flatheadbeacon.com/articles/article/flathead_electric_cooperative_at_forefront_of_renewable_energy/12635 (accessed March 17, 2010).

Reed, John. "Carmakers Tempt Mobile Phone Generation with Pay-as-You-Go." *Financial Times*, May 7, 2010. http://www.ft.com/cms/s/0/dba162ba-5980-11df-99ba-00144feab49a.html (accessed May 12, 2010).

Ries, Eric. "Marching through Quicksand." *Lessons Learned*, August 24, 2009. http://www.startuplessonslearned.com/2009/08/marching-through-quicksand.html (accessed March 17, 2010).

Rifkin, Jeremy. *The Empathic Civilization: The Race to Global Consciousness in a World in Crisis*. Cambridge, England: Polity Press, 2010.

S., Paul. "Beyond Organic—Looptworks Upcycles Textile Waste into Treasures." *TriplePundit*, September 4, 2009, http://www.triplepundit.com/2009/09/beyond-organic-looptworks-upcycles-textile-waste-into-treasures (accessed March 17, 2010).

Sachs, Jeffrey D. *Common Wealth: Economics for a Crowded Planet*. New York: Penguin Press, 2008.

Setzer, Glenn. "House Swaps—Not Just for Vacationers Anymore?" *Mortgage News Daily*, February 20, 2008, http://www.mortgagenewsdaily.com/2202008_Permanent_House_Swap.asp (accessed March 17, 2010).

Siegler, M. G. "Twitter Can Now Know Where You Tweet." *TechCrunch*, August 20, 2009, http://www.techcrunch.com/2009/08/20/twitter-can-now-know-where-you-tweet (accessed March 17, 2010).

Sunstein, Cass R., and Richard H. Thaler. *Nudge: Improving Decisions about Health, Wealth, and Happiness*. New York: Caravan, 2008.

"Survive in '09: Neighborhood Sharing on the Rise." CBS3, August 26, 2009, http://cbs3.com/topstories/sharing.neighborhood.survive.2.1145308.html (accessed March 16, 2010).

Taylor, Tanis. "Meet the Urban Sharecroppers." *Guardian*, September 4, 2008, http://www.guardian.co.uk/environment/2008/sep/04/ethicalliving.organics (accessed March 17, 2010).

Tharoor, Shashi. *The Elephant, the Tiger, and the Cell Phone: Reflections on India—The Emerging 21st-Century Power.* New York: Arcade, 2007.

"The Year's Top Travel Sites: Check Out the 2009 Luckie Fifty." *The Social Path,* May 15, 2009, http://www.thesocialpath .com/2009/05/the-luckie-50-2009.html (accessed March 17, 2010).

"30 Ways to a Better Life." *Guardian,* January 3, 2010, http://www .guardian.co.uk/lifeandstyle/2010/jan/03/30-ways-to-improve-your-life (accessed March 17, 2010).

"This Weekend: Spring Seed Swap in Woodlawn, Tree Stewardship Workshop in Concordia." Sentinel, February 26, 2010, http://portlandsentinel.com/node/5936 (accessed March 17, 2010).

Tobin, Lucy. "Power, Pilates and Tango to the People." *Guardian,* November 11, 2008, http://www.guardian.co.uk/education/ 2008/nov/11/school-of-everything-education (accessed March 16, 2010).

Tupper, Peter. "Why Comox Valley Is Launching Its Own Currency." *The Tyee,* August 14, 2009, http://thetyee.ca/News/2009/08/14/ ComoxValleyCurrency (accessed March 17, 2010).

"UK Travel News Roundup." *Guardian,* November 14, 2009, http://www.guardian.co.uk/travel/2009/nov/14/travel-news-roundup-14-nov (accessed March 17, 2010).

Upham, B. C. "Democratization of Electricity: Are You a Public Utility?" *TriplePundit,* October 29, 2009, http://www.triplepundit .com/2009/10/democratization-of-electricity-are-you-a-public-utility (accessed March 17, 2010).

Vaitheeswaran, Vijay V. *Power to the People: How the Coming Energy Revolution Will Transform an Industry, Change Our Lives, and Maybe Even Save the Planet.* New York: Farrar, Straus and Giroux, 2003.

Vance, Ashlee. "Open Source as a Model for Business Is Elusive." *New York Times,* November 30, 2009, http://www.nytimes

.com/2009/11/30/technology/business-computing/30open .html (accessed March 17, 2010).

Von Lunen, Jacques. "Pet Talk: Portland's New Pet Food Bank Was Decades in the Making." *Oregon Live*, November 2009, http:// www.oregonlive.com/pets/index.ssf/2009/11/portlands_new _pet_food_bank_wa.html (accessed March 17, 2010).

Walljasper, Jay. *Things We Share: A Field Guide to the Commons*. New York: New Press, 2010.

Warren, Georgia, and Robert Watts. "Mail Strikes Spawn Cheaper Rivals." *Times*, November 8, 2009, http://business.time sonline.co.uk/tol/business/industry_sectors/support_services/ article6908088.ece (accessed March 17, 2010).

Weiner, Eric. *The Geography of Bliss: One Grump's Search for the Happiest Places in the World*. New York: Hachette, 2008.

Wilson, Edward O. *The Diversity of Life*. New York: Norton, 1993.

Index